TUDOR TAXATION RECORDS: A GUIDE FOR USERS

by

R W Hoyle

PRO Publications

PRO Publications

Chancery Lane

London

WC2A 1LR

© Crown Copyright 1994

ISBN 1 873162 11 1

TUDOR TAXATION RECORDS:

A GUIDE FOR USERS

Frontispiece

The head of the 1524 lay subsidy return for York and the Ainsty (E179/217/92). This is a splendid example of one of the first generation of lay subsidy rolls although unusual in format, being written in five columns. It was also amongst the earliest to be published. The head of the roll announces that it is the schedule indented referred to in the indenture with the high collectors which is sewn to the bottom of the return. Both are dated 9 April 15 Henry VIII [1524]. The return for the city is subdivided into wards, each of which has its own total. The present illustration conveys no sense of the size of the manuscript which is about 2' broad and 8' 6" long.

CONTENTS

Plates and Maps			vii
Introduction			viii
A note on dates			ix
A note on manuscripts			x
1		Types of Taxes	1
2		Records of the Fifteenth	6
3		Records of Lay Subsidies	8
	i	Location	8
	ii	Coverage	9
	iii	What was taxed	12
	iv	The procedures for assessing a subsidy	16
	v	Records of the Lay Subsidy	21
	vi	The later Lay Subsidies	26
	vii	Anticipations	31
	viii	Certificates of Residence	32
	ix	The enrolled accounts and other Exchequer records	34
4		Records of Benevolences and Loans	37
	i	Prerogative taxes	38
	ii	Forced Loans	39

iii   The Military Survey of 1522 and the Forced Loans of 1522-1523   42

iv   The records of the later loans   47

v   Appendix: Records of the Military Survey of 1522 and the loans
          of 1522-1523   49

5   Finding the nominal return you require   54

6   A bibliography of Tax Returns in print   62

PLATES

Frontispiece   The Lay Subsidy return for the City of York and the Ainsty, 1524

1a and 1b   The Lay Subsidy return for All Saints Pavement, York, 1524, and
its transcript   11

2a and 2b   Goring, Oxfordshire, the township's 'bill', October 1516, and the estreat
given to the subcollectors, 14 October 1516   19, 20

3   Wigston Magna, Leicestershire, the first part of the 1524 Lay Subsidy
return   27

4   Wigston Magna, Leicestershire, the 1600 Lay Subsidy return   28

5   A privy seal for a forced loan, 1589   40

6   The Berkshire Military Survey, 1522   44

7   Decay and the Lay Subsidy, Ripon, Yorkshire, 1545   55

MAPS

1   Taxable Population in England, 1524-1525, showing areas lacking returns   56

2   Taxable Population in England, 1543-5, showing areas lacking returns   57

INTRODUCTION

To call a book 'Tudor Taxation Records: a guide for users' begs two inevitable and unavoidable questions. Who are the users? And why do they require a guide? Amongst the categories of records described here, the lay subsidy returns have been a standard source for local historians for over a century. Virtually all modern local histories contain a reference to - if not a transcript of - one or other of the 1524-1525 returns. Genealogists too have relied heavily on the returns as lists of names in which their ancestors can be located. Economic historians and historical geographers, who were perhaps slow to discover the utility of the rolls, have drawn on them in studies of the geographical and social distribution of wealth. Latterly the subsidy rolls, again especially those of 1524-1525, have been used as the basis of calculations of population size. There are then several constituencies of researchers using these records in studies of place, people and prosperity. This guide is intended to help all of them by directing researchers to the sources which may assist them most, and by offering the essential background to aid them to understand the evidence they see before them.

But there are more records of Tudor taxation than the lay subsidy returns, many of which need to be better appreciated. Moreover, I have been encouraged to write this guide out of the conviction that the records of taxation are more complicated and less easy to handle than is often allowed. They deserve consideration and description as the end-products of complex administrative processes. For these various reasons the guide is not simply an account of the nominal returns, the 'lay subsidy rolls', to which most historians are drawn. It is a description of the forms of taxation available to the state (as opposed to the borough or parish) in the sixteenth century, the procedures employed to collect the tax and the records which arose from the collection and accounting of the tax. The guide makes no pretence to be a manual of the uses to which the evidence contained in the records might be put nor, within a short scope, can it list the records themselves. It tries to distil the practical experience of a decade of using, writing about and editing these records. The guide also draws heavily on the scholarship of those who have trodden these paths before, in particular Julian Cornwall and Roger Schofield.

Preston

1 December 1993

A note on dates

The conventions by which a lay subsidy is described are confused. Three possible means of dating can be offered:

- the date of the session of parliament which granted the subsidy or fifteenth. Normally several subsidies and fifteenths were granted together. Contemporaries therefore spoke of (say) the third subsidy granted in 14 Henry VIII. We can talk of the subsidies (or the first, second, etc subsidy) granted in 1523 and make the description wholly unambiguous by citing the statute, in this case 14 & 15 Henry VIII, c.16. Elizabethan subsidies were divided into two payments separated by some months, hence (for instance) 'the second payment of the third subsidy granted in 39 Elizabeth';

- the date for the completion of assessment laid down in the statute;

- the date at which payment of the subsidy monies was due at the Exchequer.

The date of assessment and the date for payment into the Exchequer sometimes fall either side of the beginning of the modern calendar year. With the subsidies granted in 1523, the convention is to take the date at which the money was delivered to the Exchequer, so the subsidies become 1524, 1525, 1526 and 1527. The best convention for the three subsidies granted in 1543 is to take the date of assessment (1543, 1544, 1545) rather than the date of delivery (6 February 1544, 1545, 1546). This avoids confusion with the subsidies granted in 1545, the first of which was due to be received at the Exchequer on 1 April 1546. Alternatively (and this is sometimes seen), the two subsidies due to be paid in early 1546 can be distinguished by reference to the statute, so 1546 ('43) and 1546 ('45).

The use of regnal years to describe a subsidy should always be avoided (see p 60 below). Apart from this, it matters less which convention is followed than that it is always made clear to the reader which subsidy is intended.

A note on manuscripts

All the records mentioned in this guide (with a few exceptions) are in the custody of the Public Record Office (hereafter PRO) at its repository at Chancery Lane, London, WC2A 1LR. The Office is open Monday to Friday, 9.30am - 5.00pm except on public holidays and during Stocktaking which is usually the first two full weeks of October in each year.

On the completion of the new Public Record Office at Kew in the late 1990s, all will be transferred there.

1. TYPES OF TAXES

Justly it is said that the past is another country. In the sixteenth century there was no regular direct taxation on behalf of the state. Taxation was an extraordinary source of revenue, called upon to assist the monarch in bearing an extraordinary burden of expenditure, normally war or the preparation for war. It was therefore intermittent rather than regular and the dates at which it was granted and collected are broadly those in which England was engaged in war. The relationship between war and taxation appears to break down in the reign of Elizabeth I, but it may be seen clearly in the reign of Henry VIII. Here there are three periods of heavy taxation, 1512-1516, 1522-1525 and 1542-1547, each of which coincides with a period of Henry's martial adventures in a foreign theatre of war. Most years in Elizabeth's reign saw the collection of some form of taxation, whether fifteenths or subsidies. Whilst this has been claimed to be 'peacetime' taxation, it is arguable that the crown's income from taxes over the reign fell short of its military expenditure.

The taxes that the crown had at its disposal fall into two categories: firstly, taxes granted by parliament, of which there were two types, fifteenths and lay subsidies; secondly, prerogative taxes, a range of grants and benevolences. For convenience forced loans will be considered under this same heading. The records of each of these taxes will be treated in turn (chapters 2 - 4): here we will describe how they differed.[1]

Lay subsidies and fifteenths were normally granted together and for a set number of years, as in 1534 where two subsidies were granted to be collected in the autumn of 1535 and 1536 with a fifteenth to be collected in 1537. Whilst superficially simi-

---

[1]   This guide does not concern itself with the records of clerical taxation.

lar, the fifteenth and the subsidy need to be firmly distinguished. The fifteenth, as it was collected in the sixteenth century, was a quota tax. The lay subsidy in the later thirteenth and early fourteenth century had been levied on the wealth discovered by the individual assessment of taxpayers in the same way as the lay subsidy of the sixteenth century. The tax rate varied between town and countryside, the rates in the years after 1332 being normally a tenth in boroughs and ancient demesne manors and a fifteenth in rural areas. Because each subsidy (until that of 1332) was made on a new assessment of taxpayers and potentially at a different rate, the yield varied from subsidy to subsidy. From 1334 the principle of individual assessment was abandoned. In its place the commissioners charged with the collection of the subsidy were instructed to negotiate with each community for the payment of a sum of tax not less than that received in 1332. How the community raised the sum was a matter for each individual place. This was successful in that the subsidy of 1334 raised £37,450 where that of 1332 had raised £34,296. In 1336 the tax collectors were told to demand from each community the sum they had paid in 1334. The 1334 quotas then formed the basis of the fifteenth until the seventeenth century. The crown was spared the problem of making an assessment for each subsidy, but over time the system of fixed quotas ceased to match the distribution of wealth. The desertion or partial depopulation of communities posed especial problems, and in the fifteenth century a total of £6,000 was divided amongst the counties as an allowance to be used to reduce the quotas of those places which were no longer able to pay their fifteenth. These allowances were still being credited when the fifteenth was last collected in 1623.[2]

As government was not interested in who paid the fifteenth, merely that the correct monies should be received, it made no attempt to ensure that it was paid by the

---

[2]   For taxation in the early fourteenth century, see most conveniently M Ormrod, 'The crown and the English Economy, 1290-1348', in B M S Campbell (ed), *Before the Black Death. Studies in the 'crisis' of the early fourteenth century (1991)*. The 1334 values are printed in R E Glasscock, *The Lay Subsidy of 1334* (British Academy Records of Social and Economic History, new series, II, 1975). The local distribution of the reductions of the fifteenth made in the fifteenth century may be of interest, see D Dymond and R Virgoe, 'The reduced population and wealth of early fifteenth-century Suffolk', *Proceedings of the Suffolk Institute of Archaeology and History*, XXXVI (1985-8), pp 73-100.

richest members of the community. There is a great deal of scattered comment which suggests that the fifteenth was often spread as broadly as possible within each community, with the wealthiest paying a disproportionately small part. This was alleged within a few years of the introduction of the quota system.[3] In 1603 a preacher at St Paul's Cross in London could complain of the oppression of the poor by the fifteenth 'wherein the burden is more heavy upon a mechanical or handicraft poor man than upon an alderman'. In Moulton, Lincolnshire, in the same year, it was claimed that the fifteenth was raised by first assessing those 'strangers and foreigners' having land or cattle within the parish, after which the inhabitants made up any shortfall.[4]

The Tudor lay subsidy was a revival of the medieval practice of making individual assessments. Direct taxes of any sort were rarely granted in the fifteenth century and the lay subsidy, as it came to be used in the century after 1523, was very much an invention of the 1510s (although there is evidence that these subsidies were not seen to be successes at the time).[5] The essential features of the Tudor lay subsidy were, firstly, that it was a tax on individuals whose liability was decided by thresholds and scales laid down in the statute. Secondly, the tax was open ended in that there was no fixed quota to be met by the parish or county. The numbers of persons taxed and the overall yield could be increased or diminished by modifying the scales and thresholds contained in the statutes. So, the first two of the four subsidies granted in 1523 included within their nets all with more than £1 in lands, £2 in goods or £1 in wages, but the second two included only those with more than £50 in lands (in 1526) or goods (in 1527). Hence the size of the subsidy roll varied enormously from subsidy to subsidy. Aliens were also taxed, normally at a disadvantageous rate. The third rule was that a taxpayer only paid once and in his normal place of residence, but he was charged there with all his lands and goods

---

3   Ormrod, 'Crown and English Economy', p 157.

4   Cited by I W Archer, *The pursuit of stability. Social relations in Elizabethan London* (1991), p 53; J Thirsk and J P Cooper ed *Seventeenth Century Economic Documents* (1972), p 603.

5   The development of the lay subsidy is most fully described in R S Schofield, 'Parliamentary Lay Taxation, 1485-1547' (Cambridge PhD thesis, 1963), ch 4. This is the fullest account of the administration of early Tudor taxation, which all serious students will wish to consult. Again, I am pleased to acknowledge my debt to it.

within the realm and not merely those lying within that township or parish.

There is then a basic difference between the subsidy and the fifteenth. In the fifteenth the Exchequer told the commissioners how much to collect and did not enquire how the money was raised. With the subsidy, the Exchequer had to be warned how much to expect and wished to know that the assessment had been conducted according to the provisions of the statute. The records of the two taxes are therefore quite different.

Akin to the subsidy is the relief, a parliamentary tax of which three payments were granted in 1548 and a fourth in 1549. The relief is in reality a subsidy which for political reasons could not be so called. It differs from the subsidy only in that lands were not taxed.

The prerogative taxes are much less well known and their records are scattered and fragmentary.[6] A benevolence, broadly speaking, was a tax raised on the authority of the royal prerogative (rather than by statute). In theory (though not in practice) benevolences had been outlawed by statute of 1484. The most important prerogative tax in the sixteenth century, strictly defined, is the Benevolence of 1545. The Amicable Grant of 1525, had it been implemented, would have more than matched it in the demands it made on taxpayers.[7] Forced loans were loans taken from individual taxpayers with a promise of repayment. Great trouble was taken to make it appear that such loans were voluntary, but in truth, those declining to lend or offering a smaller sum than they were thought able to lend stood to be threatened by admonishing letters or be called before the council. Their payment was, in reality, coerced. Most Elizabethan forced loans were repaid, but others, including the loans taken in 1522-1523 and 1544, were retrospectively converted into grants by statute.[8] The most exhaustive forced loans were those of

6   For these taxes in general and their medieval antecedents, G L Harriss, 'Aids, Loans and Benevolences', *Historical Journal*, VI (1963), pp 1-19.

7   For the Amicable Grant, see G W Bernard, *War, Taxation and Rebellion in early Tudor England* (1986); G W Bernard and R W Hoyle, 'The instructions for the levying of the Amicable Grant, March 1525' forthcoming in *Historical Research* LXVII (1994).

8   21 Henry VIII c.24; 35 Henry VIII, c.12.

1522-1523 which followed on the preparation of military and fiscal assessments in 1522, the so-called 'Military Surveys'. The surveys, where they survive, are potentially of great interest to the historian and are described at length in chapter 4.

The greater part of the records of these various forms of taxation in the PRO have been included in the class of 'Subsidy Rolls etc', E 179. This class was put together by the nineteenth-century arrangers of the public records along lines which contravene all the modern rules of archival arrangement. The class contains taxation records drawn from many different periods and sources, broadly from the twelfth century to the seventeenth. It includes both records produced locally and submitted to the Exchequer and documents produced as a part of the accounting process within the Exchequer. Not surprisingly, it is a large class containing some 30,000 documents arranged in first county and then chronological order. This guide, though, is not simply a description of a section of E 179, but an aid to discovering and understanding the records of taxation wherever they may be found, both in the PRO and outside.

2. RECORDS OF THE FIFTEENTH

There are relatively few records of the fifteenth extant which will aid the local historian or genealogist. Those which are of interest are as likely to be found in local archives as within the PRO. There are, for instance, lists of those who contributed to sixteenth-century fifteenths for Nottingham, Winchester and Southampton, but they survive amongst the towns' own archives. Assessments for the fifteenth in Colchester are in the manuscript collections of the British Library.[1] Copies of 'rentals' or rate lists which identify the parcels of land liable to pay the tax are occasionally discovered. An example in the PRO is an assessment for Eddlesborough, Buckinghamshire, of 1512-1513. Another Buckinghamshire assessment, for the fifteenth of 1512-1513 charged on Emberton, has been printed, as has one of 1599 for Cowden, Kent.[2]

The larger part of the materials in E 179 are copies of the 'particulars of account' or *Particule Compoti*, the list supplied to the collectors of the fifteenth, which gives for each parish or township the sum due in 1334, the deduction for decays and the sum payable in tax. For the names of the collectors of the tax, turn to the enrolled accounts in E 359. But in the normal run of things, it is impossible to discover who paid the fifteenth unless the levying of the tax prompted a dispute.

On this special matter the PRO has a scattering of materials which are of interest to the historian of taxation or, if he or she is fortunate enough to discover it, the local historian. Dr Schofield supplies a list of disputes 1485-1547 in his thesis, most of which are drawn from the Exchequer Memoranda Rolls (E 359), but they are relatively few in number. An illustrative case is in print.[3] A few equitable cases in E 111 (early Exchequer bills and answers) turn on the liability of hamlets or tithings to contribute with other

---

1   *Records of the Borough of Nottingham*, ed W H Stevenson and others, (9 vols, London, etc, 1882-1956), IV, pp 240-242, 293-296; Tom Atkinson, *Elizabethan Winchester* (1963), pp 136-137; *The Hampshire Lay Subsidy Rolls, 1586 ...*, ed C R Davey, (Hampshire Record Series IV, 1981), pp 114-119; *The Assembly Books of Southampton*, I, ed J W Horrocks, (Southampton Record Series, XIX, 1917), pp 1-23; Colchester, British Library, Stowe Mss 828 (late fifteenth century), 830 (27-32 Elizabeth).

2   E 179/387/9; *Early Taxation Returns*, ed A C Chibnall, (Buckinghamshire Record Series, XIV, 1966), pp 108-109; 'Assessment of the parish of Cowden [Kent], AD 1599', *Archaeologia Cantiana*, XI (1877), pp 392-393.

3   Schofield, 'Parliamentary Lay Taxation', table 7, pp 93-94; *Surrey Taxation Returns* II (Surrey Record Series, XXXIII, 1932), pp lxxvi, 176-179 (Withey, Surrey, 1561).

townships: these cases mostly date from the 1540s. Later cases of this sort may be found in the Exchequer Equity Pleadings (E 112), but a search of the Yorkshire pleadings to 1625 shows that they are few in number. Disputes over the levying of the fifteenth may also be found in other courts, with Henrician cases concerning Barnstaple (Devon) and Burford (Oxfordshire) in Star Chamber.[4] Generally speaking though, this is unrewarding territory.

The records of the collection of the fifteenth and the discharge of collectors made within the Exchequer are similar to those made for the lay subsidy and are described in chapter 3 **(ix)** below.

---

[4]   STAC 2/3, ff 289-302; 7, ff 51r-62v.

3. RECORDS OF LAY SUBSIDIES

The taxation records most heavily and profitably drawn upon by historians and genealogists are the nominal returns of persons paying the lay subsidy. This chapter explains how the subsidy was levied and describes the whole range of records made as a part of its assessment and collection.

(i) Location

The majority of the surviving lay subsidy returns are found in the Public Record Office in class E 179. The survival of lay subsidy returns there is, however, far from perfect, nor is the PRO the only place where original lay subsidy returns may be discovered.

In his account of the making of a lay subsidy in the 1620s, Henry Best of Elmswell in the East Riding of Yorkshire describes how copies of earlier returns were kept by the *custos rotulorum* of the county to allow the new roll to be compared against the old.[1] So far as can be ascertained, no quarter sessions archive contains lay subsidy rolls lodged with the Clerk of the Peace for this purpose. Rolls or copies of rolls do survive in municipal archives, perhaps because record keeping was better in towns than counties. At York, the city's records include a series of registers containing copies of the returns for the city and the Ainsty throughout the later sixteenth century.[2] Other rolls or copies of rolls may be found from time to time in estate collections deposited in local record offices. They also appear in collections formed by the early county historians, for lay subsidy rolls, giving as they do the names of the inhabitants of a county, were of as great an interest to antiquarians of an earlier generation as to us. Occasionally returns may be

---

[1] *The Farming and Memorandum Books of Henry Best of Elmswell* ed D Woodward, (British Academy Records of Social and Economic History, new series VIII, 1984), pp 91-92.

[2] York City Archives Dept, E48-51, E59, E59A.

found in local record offices which predate the series now in the PRO.

A few examples of this may be offered from Yorkshire materials. The West Yorkshire Archive Service recently purchased an incomplete collector's roll for the wapentake of Osgoldcross for 1472. Another return which predates the series in the Exchequer's archive is a return for the subsidy of 1489 for Claro Wapentake, which survives in a copy made by the seventeenth-century antiquary Roger Dodsworth now in the Bodleian Library. Another collector's roll, for the liberty of Ripon for the subsidy of 1524, may be found in the records of the Middleton family of Stockeld at the Yorkshire Archaeological Society, Leeds. A copy of the roll for the wapentakes of Osgoldcross, Barkston, Staincross and Skyrack for 1585 may be found in the antiquarian collections of Nathaniel Johnston, also in the Bodleian.[3]

Documents held in local record offices may be extremely important for filling gaps in the series of returns in the PRO. Even where they appear to duplicate records in the PRO, they may provide readings of sections which are illegible in the PRO copy. For this reason the assiduous student should search them out. But they are few in number compared to the large numbers in the custody of the PRO.

(ii) Coverage

The lay subsidy returns cover the whole of England with the exception of the Cinque Ports and the four northern counties. There are no returns for Cheshire or Wales as a whole before 1542.

The native born inhabitants of the Cinque Ports and their rural hundreds were invariably exempted from paying the subsidy. The returns for these towns in E 179 are

---

[3] West Yorkshire Archive Service, Wakefield Office, C654; Bodleian Library, Ms Dodsworth 50, ff. 39r-79r; Yorkshire Archaeological Society, Leeds, MD59/19/39; Bodleian Library, Ms Top. Yorks. c.45, ff. 70r-86v.

for aliens inhabiting there. Brighton was excused the payment of the subsidy in 1515, 1516 and 1524-1527 but not thereafter. Ludlow was exempted in 1524-1527. There are other minor exemptions in other statutes, normally to take account of natural calamities.

The special situation in the North must be explained. Cumberland, Westmorland and Northumberland were traditionally excused the payment of parliamentary taxes because of the costs they faced in defending England against the Scots. After 1603, upon the unification of the crowns of England and Scotland, this concession lapsed. The earliest lay subsidy rolls on the denizens of these counties are therefore those from the first years of the reign of James I. The subsidy returns dated before this in E 179, including those of the relief, are actually returns of aliens - Scots - resident in the counties who were liable to be taxed under all statutes from 1534 onwards. The counties did pay the benevolence of 1545 but sadly there are no extant records.[4] The situation in county Durham is rather obscure. The county, because of its palatinate status, did not pay parliamentary taxes although, again, aliens within the county were taxed.

Wales, here including Monmouth, did not pay subsidies until the 1543 subsidy which was the first granted after the shiring of Wales in 1541. Nor did the parts of Hereford and Shropshire which were added to those counties when Wales was shired. After 1541 there was no distinction between the taxation of English counties and Welsh counties. The earliest (and fullest) returns for Wales should be the returns to the statute of 1543, but these survive imperfectly.

Cheshire was exempted from the statutes before and including that of 1523.

One final matter should be mentioned. The subsidy was administered by commissioners authorised by Chancery. Each county or borough had a single commission, but other, separate commissions were issued for the assessment and taxing of the royal

---

4   G R Batho ed, *A calendar of the Talbot Papers in the College of Arms* (Derbyshire Record Series, IV, 1971), p 350 (comments on the problems of assessing the benevolence in Cumberland without subsidy rolls).

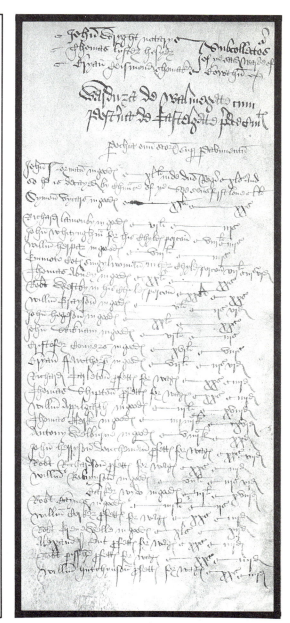

John Wryght notary
Thomas Lyster hosier   } Subcollectors of the said
Bryan Teismond shomaker } warde of Bowthum.

WARDURA DE WALMEGATE CUM POSTERNA DE
CASTELGATE PREDICTE CIVITATIS.

PAROCHIA OMNIUM SANCTORUM
SUPER PAVIMENTUM,

John Norman in goods 40*l*., inde Dño Regi	40*s*.	0*d*.
And so he is decayed by chaunce of ye see sens first leve 50*l*.		
Symon Vycars in goods 20*l*.	20*s*.	0*d*.
Richard Lamonby in goods 6*l*.	3*s*.	0*d*.
John Whityngham for his chylds porcon 8*l*.	4*s*.	0*d*.
William Herpar in goods 8*l*.	4*s*.	0*d*.
Emmote Cotes singylwoman in her chylds porcon 7*l*.	3*s*.	6*d*.
Thomas Abney in goods 20*l*.	20*s*.	0*d*.
Robert Westby in his chylds porcon 20*l*.	20*s*.	0*d*.
William Grayson in goods 5*l*.	2*s*.	6*d*.
John Hogeson in goods 20*l*.	20*s*.	0*d*.
John Stiknam in goods 6*l*.	3*s*.	0*d*.
Cristofer Conyers in goods 16*l*.	8*s*.	0*d*.
Bryan Fawthorp in goods 7*l*.	3*s*.	6*d*.
Richard Carleton profetts for wages 20*s*.		4*d*.
Thomas Shipton profetts for wages 20*s*.		4*d*.
William Appilgarth in goods 3*l*.		18*d*.
Thomas Clerk in goods 4 marks		16*d*.
Antony Welburne in goods 5 marks		20*d*.
John Herryson Doucheman profetts for wages 20*s*.		8*d*.
Robert Rychardson profetts for wages 20*s*.		4*d*.
William Robynson in goods 7*l*.	3*s*.	6*d*.
Barker wydo in goods 3*l*.		18*d*.
Robert Baynes in goods 4*l*.	2*s*.	0*d*.
William Corker profetts for wages 20*s*.		4*d*.
Robert Grenewelle in goods 40*s*.		12*d*.
Alexander Kent profetts for wages 20*s*.		4*d*.
Robert Parisshe profetts for wages 20*s*.		4*d*.
William Hutchynson profetts for wages 20*s*.		4*d*.

Plates 1a (left) **and 1b** (right)

The 1524 return for All Saints Pavement in the City of York (E179/219/96) with its transcript. This is a detail from the roll shown in the frontispiece and illustrates the typical layout of the lay subsidy. At the head of the plate are the names of the subcollectors for Bootham ward, then a heading for Walmgate ward and the parish heading. Each entry gives the name of the taxpayers, the nature of his or her tax assessment, its value and the tax paid. The first assessment, for John Norman, explains that his wealth has diminished by £50 since the making of the military survey 'by chance of the seas'. John Whityngham, Emma Cotes singlewoman and others were taxed on their child's portion. Others were taxed on their 'profit for wages' paying 4d a piece except for John Herryson, 'doucheman', who, as an alien, paid at double the normal rate. The assessment continues at the head of the next column and ends with the assessment of Corpus Christi Guild.

household(s), the nobility and (in 1524-1527) the Cardinal's household. The returns of nobles and the household form a distinct section of E 179 and in the typescript calendar the appropriate list will be found after the Welsh counties. It is not impossible that some persons, especially gentry, who appear to be missing from the assessments for their normal place of residence, may have been taxed as a member of one or other households.

(iii) What was taxed

Taxpayers could be assessed on one of three categories of wealth: income from lands or other income (conventionally and misleadingly referred to as 'lands'), goods or wages.[5] Not all categories of wealth were taxed in every subsidy. For instance, there were no assessments on wages made after the subsidy granted in 1523 (and then wages were assessed only in 1524 and 1525). No lands were assessed by the reliefs of 1548-1551. The exact definitions of the categories of taxable wealth were amended over time. The following discussion is based on the earlier statutes but, as will appear, changes in the exact definitions may be ignored.

> Lands were defined in the 1523 statute as being
>
> ... that [which] the same person or other to his use have in fee simple, fee tail, term of life, term of years, execution, by ward, by copy of court roll or at will, in any castle, honour, manor, lands, tenements, rents, services, hereditaments, annuities, fees, corrodies or profits of the very just and clear yearly value thereof ...

This makes it clear that the assessment was on income rather than capital value. As the majority of income was drawn from lands, most 'lands' assessments are a reflection of the rental value of the taxpayer's lands (less deductions). There is some evidence that in 1524 the rentals of peers were inspected by the commissioners charged with their

5   For a fuller discussion of these matters, see Schofield, 'Parliamentary Lay Taxation', pp 238-244.

assessment but, taking the century as a whole, this was not normal practice.[6] A small minority of persons paid on fees and annuities: these are often distinguished within the subsidy rolls.

Goods were defined in the same statute as being either coin or that which

> any such person hath of his own in plate, stock of merchandise, all manner of corns and blades severed from the ground, household stuff and all other goods and chattels moveable as well within this realm as without, and of all such sums of money that to him is owing, whereof he trusteth in his conscience surely to be paid, except ... such sums of money as he oweth and in his conscience surely to pay and except also apparell of all persons belonging to their bodies, saving jewels of gold.[7]

The definition therefore excludes standing corn but includes the stock of merchants and retailers, clothing and money out at loan (although it also allowed a taxpayer's debts to be credited against his assets). This may be thought to favour the arable farmer against the pastoral. It is noticeable, though, that most early Tudor subsidies were assessed and levied towards the end of the year after the harvest (and when liquidity would have been greatest).

The implications of the two definitions are that the subsidy taxed the *income* from one form of capital asset (land) whilst in the case of goods it taxed the *capital* value of the asset rather than the profits generated by it. This may have been a matter of convenience, for verifying the profit received from a farming or commercial enterprise was beyond the ability of government even if those figures could ever have been secured. The economic significance of this distinction is immense. It might even be suggested that it was advantageous for the merchant to move his assets into lands or even annuities charged on lands to reduce his tax liabilities.

Wages, the final category, were only taxed in the earlier Henrician subsidies and

---

6   H Miller, 'Subsidy assessments of the peerage in the sixteenth century', *Bulletin of the Institute of Historical Research*, XXVIII (1955), pp 24-26.

7   *Statutes of the Realm*, III, p 231.

never after 1525 (except and insofar as they might be counted as income).

Various points arise from this which need to be digested if the working of the subsidy is to be fully comprehended. Each taxpayer only paid on one category of taxable wealth. This was not a matter of election, but was decided (for the small number of individuals for whom the question might arise) by calculating which type of wealth, when taxed, brought the crown the greatest revenue. So, if a taxpayer is assessed on goods, we cannot assume that he had no lands, but we can (in theory at least) make a calculation of how small his lands must have been to compel his taxation on goods.

There also appears to have been a convention that the tenants of copyhold lands or leasehold lands did not have those lands included within their assessment. This appears very clearly in the 1522 military surveys where we have assessments for both 'lands' and goods. In virtually every case, men holding lands at rent are given a nil 'lands' assessment.[8] Of course lands which the taxpayer held for rent did not produce an 'income', for, as the definition reveals, this was thought of in terms of a money rent or fee. The reason may also be that to tax copyholders or lessees on the lands they held as tenants and landowners on their income from the same lands would be to introduce a form of double taxation.

Taxation on the lowest land assessment in the later subsidies is actually a form of tax avoidance and may not indicate the possession of land at all. The standard rates in the later Elizabethan subsidies were that persons worth £1 or more in lands paid 4s in the pound in two payments of 2s 8d and 1s 4d. For goods, the threshold was £3 and the rate 2s 8d in the pound, split into two uneven payments of 1s 8d and 1s. The smallest goods payment was therefore 5s for the first payment and 3s for the second (making 8s in all). It was therefore advantageous for the taxpayer to secure an assessment at £1 lands and

8   The *Military Survey of Gloucestershire, 1522*, ed R W Hoyle, (Gloucestershire Record Series, VI, 1993), pp xviii-xxi.

pay the very minimum contribution to the subsidy. This practice was sometimes widespread and is one of the most obvious symptoms of the deteriorating efficiency of the subsidy. In York, over 10 per cent of those contributing to the subsidy after 1595 paid on the minimum lands assessment and in 1600 almost exactly a fifth did so. Plate four shows how prevalent it was in Leicestershire at the turn of the century.

It must also be acknowledged that the values contained in the subsidy rolls are rounded estimates of wealth rather than valuations made on the view of a person's chattels. Indeed, it may be held that they describe reputed wealth rather than real wealth. Moreover, wherever an attempt has been made to correlate the subsidy valuation with other assessments of wealth for the same individuals (as in inventories or rentals), the relationship has been discovered to be weak, even in the earlier period when the subsidy was administered in an efficient manner.[9] The most elaborate attempt to cross-tabulate inventory values with subsidy assessments, by Schofield, discovered that 'the accuracy of the [subsidy] assessments declined systematically over time from 48.7% of the probate valuations in the period 1524-42 to 21.2% in the first thirteen years of Elizabeth's reign'.[10] This is in part because the assessments were made on different criteria, but also because an individual's wealth was fragile and liable to rise or fall according to his commercial success and outgoings. We would not expect a close match between a subsidy and an inventory valuation even if the two were made within a short space of time. On the other hand, Schofield's figures show beyond doubt the way in which the assessments for the subsidy become wholly untrustworthy after the end of Henry VIII's reign, a point considered further in **(v)** below. The individual assessments must be taken not as direct evidence of a person's wealth, but as an indication of how his contemporaries ranked him within his community. As Fieldhouse wrote of the return for Richmondshire,

---

9   See the attempt of R B Smith to link a rental and subsidy for Selby, Yorks., *Land and Politics in the England of Henry VIII. The West Riding of Yorkshire, 1530-1546* (1970), pp 100-103 ('... no statistical correlation can be attempted between the amount of tax a man paid and either the size of his holding, the type of tenure or even the amount he paid in rent').

10   R S Schofield, 'Taxation and the political limits of the Tudor State' in C Cross, D Loades and J J Scarisbrick ed, *Law and Government under the Tudors* (1988), pp 252-253.

'... the 1544 lay subsidy is no guide to the *total* value of a man's movable property but it does reflect the *relative* wealth and social status of the top half of the social pyramid ...'.[11]

(iv) The procedures for assessing a subsidy

The lay subsidy statute not only laid down who should contribute to the subsidy but also outlined the procedures which were to be followed in the assessment and collection of the subsidy and the date by which each stage should be completed. Implementing these instructions was the responsibility of commissioners. For the subsidies up to and including those granted in 1523, the commissioners were nominated by parliament and their names were included in a schedule annexed to the statute. In 1534 provision was made for the commissioners to be appointed by the king and in the later Henrician subsidies by a panel of the Lord Chancellor, Lord Treasurer and others.[12] The commissioners were normally gentry or borough officers, much the same sorts of person as sat on the commission of the peace. It seems likely that a senior commissioner had overall charge for calling the other commissioners together. The commissioners might also receive other letters instructing them how to proceed or enjoining them not to let the subsidy money fall in value below that collected in previous years.[13]

The commissioners normally divided themselves into subcommissions, each with charge of a hundred or several contiguous hundreds. The normal procedure was for the commissioners to issue a warrant through the head constable of the hundred calling before them representatives of every village, township or tithing. At this meeting a charge was read which explained why it was necessary to raise a tax, who was liable to be

---

[11] R Fieldhouse, 'Social structures from Tudor lay subsidy and probate inventories: a case study: Richmondshire, Yorkshire', *Local Population Studies*, 12 (1974), p 18 (italics as in the original).

[12] Schofield, 'Parliamentary Lay Taxation', p 200 offers fuller details. Lists of commissioners in print can be found as follows: *Statutes of the Realm*, III, pp 79-89 (1513), 112-119 (1514), 168-175 (1515-1516), then *Letters and Papers of Henry VIII* (hereafter *Letters and Papers*), III, no 3,283 (1524) and IV (i), no 547 (1525). Rolls of the names of commissioners can be found in E 179/280 (broadly fourteenth-fifteenth century) and E 179/281 (four rolls, all but one undated, broadly Henrician).

[13] For examples of such letters, see 'Letters of the Cliffords, lords Clifford and earls of Cumberland, c1500-c1565', ed R W Hoyle, *Camden Miscellany*, XXXI (Camden 4th Series, XLIV), no 28; Lincolnshire Archives Office, L1/1/1/2 ff. 25v, 43v (1544, 1547); *Letters of the fifteenth and sixteenth centuries from the archives of Southampton* ed R C Anderson, (Southampton Record Series, XII, 1921), pp 62-66, and the letters noticed by Schofield, 'Taxation and the political limits of the Tudor state', pp 239-240.

taxed, and at what rate. Until the 1563 statute the assessors were sworn to 'truly enquire ... of the best and most value and substance of every person ... without concealment, favour, love, affection, dread, fear and malice'.[14] A day was then given at which the assessors for each township were to meet with the commissioners to return their 'bill' or list of taxpayers. The commissioners were then responsible for appointing 'petty collectors' who, armed with a copy of the list of taxpayers for their parish, collected the tax from their neighbours. The commissioners also nominated a head or high collector for each hundred. He collected the tax revenues from the petty collectors: it was his duty to see that the monies reached the Exchequer. The commissioners prepared a certificate for the Exchequer supplying the head collector's name and informing the Exchequer of the sum they should expect to receive of him.

How the bills were drawn up is largely mysterious. It has been shown that the nominal listings for Silsden (Yorkshire) are arranged topographically, for the same sequences of names (sometimes in reversed order) are found in successive returns. One may readily envisage that here at least the assessors proceeded from door to door listing the names of those liable as they proceeded.[15] Others may wish to look for clues to similar behaviour. Returns for towns are often arranged by street, again suggesting a topographical organization.

The survival of the bills (or other working papers of the commissioners) is extremely rare, although two sets survive in the PRO. E 101/699/15 is a file of paper documents from Langtree Hundred, Oxfordshire for the subsidy of 8 Henry VIII. (It probably came into the hands of the PRO with other papers of one of the commissioners, Sir Adrian Fortescue, executed in 1538.) This file contains, for a number of town-

---

14 Taken from the 1516 statute, cited by Schofield, 'Taxation and the political limits of the Tudor state', p 236.
15 I owe this to Mrs Bette Hill of Silsden.

ships, the paper bills which give the names of taxpayers and value of their assessed goods. The sum due from each taxpayer was then marked against his name in the left hand margin. For the same townships we then find the indented estreat given to the parochial collectors which provides the same list of names and the sum due. The bill and estreat for Goring is illustrated in plates 2a-b. The other set is also in a private collection now lodged in the PRO, the Duchess of Norfolk deeds. Here may be found a paper file, still on its original thong, of 23 bills for townships in Radlow hundred, Herefordshire for the first payment of the first subsidy granted in 1589. The bills, unlike the engrossed rolls, distinguish the assessors: they also reveal what cannot ever be discovered from the engrossed rolls, that the assessors' assessments were made by the commissioners. The commissioners also made other amendments to the bills, inserting the occasional name and sometimes amending the assessment. The bills do not give the tax due.[16]

It was the head collectors and not the commissioners who were responsible for the collection of the tax and the payment of the gross sums into the Exchequer. For their pains they received a poundage from the tax collected, but any shortfalls in the subsidy money were met by them and not the commissioners. Hence the collectors might be forced to petition the Exchequer for 'allowances', especially where a taxpayer had been charged in two or more hundreds. The mechanisms for avoiding this are explained in (**viii**) below.

The procedures can be quickly illustrated. When Henry Lord Cromwell received the commission for Norfolk in August 1587, he wrote to the commissioners inviting them to a meeting at the Bull at Attlebridge on the following Monday. There they apportioned responsibilities and assessed themselves. When the Cambridgeshire commissioners for the relief of 1548 gathered at Cambridge on 22 March 1549, they read the commission and the supporting letters from Protector Somerset and the council before di-

16 C 115/I29 (no 6676).

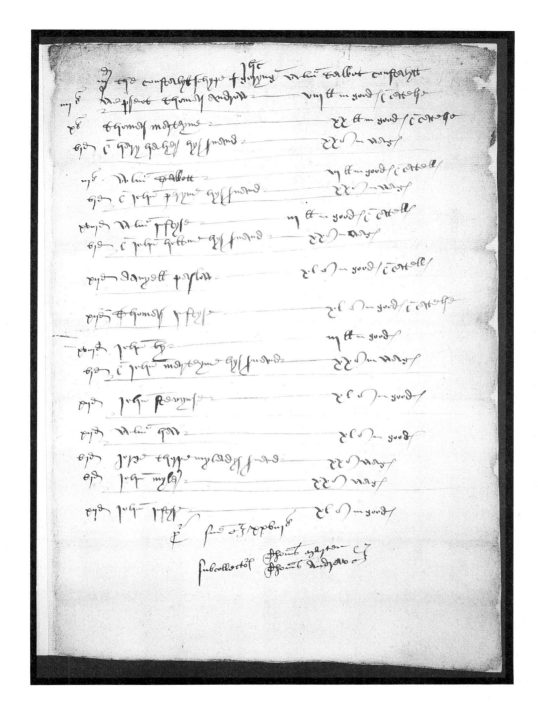

Plates 2a and 2b

The township's bill and the commissioner's estreat for Goring, Oxfordshire, October 1516, taken from a file for Langtree Hundred, Oxfordshire (E101/699/15, mm 12, 13). The list of taxpayers in the bill is clearly arranged by households (notice the horizontal lines which divide the list into ones and twos). Most of this detail is lost from the estreat although the organisation can be inferred. The individual assessments in the lefthand margin, the total and the names of the subcollectors were added to the township's bill by the commissioners. The estreat gives only the sum due and not the basis of assessment.

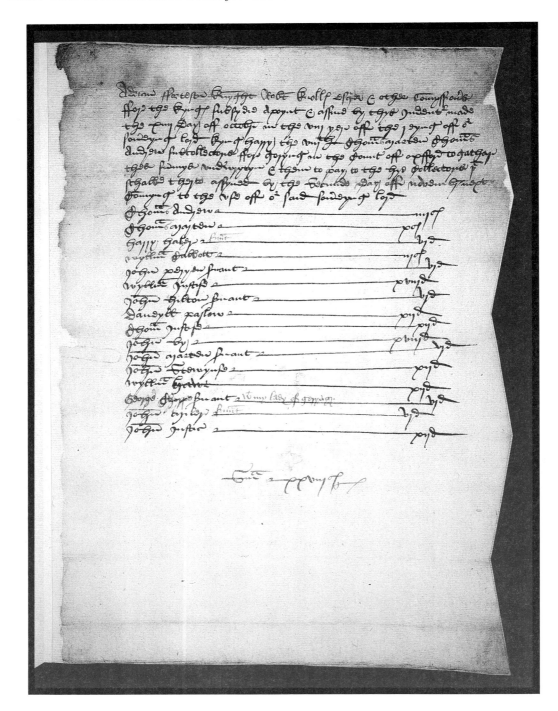

viding themselves into subcommissions. The commissioners for each wapentake then issued precepts for all township constables to attend on them on the following Monday with five of the 'most honest and substantial inhabitants of every town'. When this sizeable body of men gathered before the commissioners for the hundreds of Cheveley, Radfield, Whittleford and Chilford, their charge was read to them by Sir Edward North, three assessors for each township were chosen from those present and the date set for the return of their assessment. At Nottingham in 1599 (where events are well documented in a Star Chamber case), the township assessors appeared before the commissioners on 22 September, heard their charges and other speeches by the commissioners, and were instructed to bring their bills in two days later.[17]

It must be stressed that the commissioners neither assessed nor collected the tax (the exception being that the commissioners assessed one another). They *oversaw* the implementation of the statute, although the act provided them with powers to intervene if they thought that an individual assessment was unreasonable (whether too much or too little) and to fine any person who declined to co-operate with them. But it must also be recognised that the subsidy rolls are finally composite documents, drawn up by each parish. The reliability of a subsidy roll therefore reflects as much the determination of the commissioners to see the statute properly implemented as the anxiety of the inhabitants of each and every parish to minimize their individual contributions to the subsidy.

(v) Records of the Lay Subsidy

The study of the records produced by the lay subsidy as a whole has barely begun. Historians and genealogists have, quite understandably, focussed their attention on the

---

17 Bodleian Library, Oxford, Tanner Ms 241, ff 31r-32v; Bodleian Library, Oxford, Ms North a.1 ff 28-30; pleadings in *Attorney-General* v *Willoughby and others*, STAC 5/A15/24, STAC 5/A1/27, STAC 5/A27/32, STAC 5/A9/40.

nominal returns, but these were only one of a range of records which the commissioners had to return to the Exchequer. From 1543 onwards the records appear to be unchanging in character, but in the early years of Henry VIII's reign the Exchequer experimented with returns of increasing detail, culminating in the request that nominal returns should be sent to London.

Four major types of records can be distinguished, although not all the returns made by the commissioners fit cleanly into a single category. The first were 'divisions' or, as the typescript catalogue to E 179 called them, appointments of commissioners. These stated how the commissioners had been deployed and which of them were responsible for individual hundreds. To all appearances these were first demanded in 1524-1525. Later ones may sometimes be found stitched into the subsidy rolls. The second were certificates of assessment, the returns to the Exchequer of the names of the collectors. Thirdly, there are found in some years schedules of the payments due from individual townships. Fourthly, there are the nominal returns or estreats.

The nature of the records which the commissioners were required to send to the Exchequer was laid down in the statute supplemented by letters out of the Exchequer. In 1512 (4 Henry VIII c.14) the commissioners were to send to the Exchequer the counterpart of an indenture naming the collectors and giving the total sums with which each collector was charged. The practice in later years appears to have been to enlarge this slightly by sending to the Exchequer estreats[18] which named the sums due from each parish or other taxation unit and (in some cases) the names of the parish assessors. The crucial point is that before 1523 the commissioners were not instructed to send to the Exchequer estreats giving the names of taxpayers. The surviving records of these early subsidies are therefore pretty unprofitable for most historians and all genealogists. There

18   An estreat is a list prepared for a collector or auditor of individuals owing fines to a court or sums in taxation.

are odd certificates from the commissioners listed in the county sequence, but the majority of the returns remain in their original files and for this reason are listed under divers counties as follows: E 179/279/1, 5 Henry VIII (33 items, largely for Yorkshire); E 179/279/2, 6 Henry VIII (63 items); E 179/279/3, 7 Henry VIII (108 items). There are also similar files for the subsidies of 12 Henry VII, E 179/241/365 and 19 Henry VII, E 179/241/364.

From the subsidy granted in 1523 we have nominal returns. Why the decision was taken to have them sent to London, and by what authority, is rather mysterious. The statute (14-15 Henry VIII c.16) required the sums 'of every shire, riding, city or town ... for the subsidy to be taxed and rated yearly by the commissioners to be certified to the Exchequer' (sect. 2). More specifically, the statute ordered that after the assessing of the subsidy, the commissioners were to total up their estreats and make a writing indented containing the names of the collectors and the sums due from each collector (sect. 16). The counterparts of these indentures were to be sent to the Exchequer and the Chamber. Nowhere is it enacted that the commissioners were to send up nominal returns.

The order to do so may have been contained in a circular letter to the subsidy commissioners of late February 1524.[19] This refers to misunderstandings of the statute by which the crown stood to suffer great losses. The king had ordered the suspension of the 'entering' of the commissioners' certificates in the Exchequer until the oversights had been reformed and amended. Exactly what was required was stated in a 'memorial' which was attached, but of which no copy is extant. The letter than goes on to refer to the need to make a certificate which would testify to the commissioners' work in implementing the statute and which would include 'the particular names of every person

---

19 *Letters and Papers* IV (i) no. 122 (SP 1/30 f 142), printed from a copy in the archives of Exeter by W. Cotton, *Gleanings from the municipal and cathedral records relating to the history of the city of Exeter* (1877), pp 189-190.

within the precinct of the said commission chargeable to the said act, the valuation of their goods or lands and the sums of money wherewith they be taxed'. This clearly refers to the nominal returns with which we are familiar. The new and fuller certificates were to be delivered to the Exchequer before Easter following; until they were the collectors would not be discharged.

The statute did not require or sanction the return of certificates containing this level of detail and it is a nonsense to speak (as the letter does) of the 'inadventure and misexposition' of the act on this particular point. The lodging of nominal returns appears to be a matter of administrative fiat rather than law. And this remains the case for all the Henrician subsidies, all of which require only a certificate giving the names of the collectors and the sums for which they were responsible.

What appears to have happened in 1524 was that the commissioners sent to the Exchequer certificates similar to those made in the previous decade. In Gloucestershire we have a number of certificates dated in December 1523 or January 1524 (E 179/113/190, 114/201). There are also two returns which only give the total sums due township by township, one of which is dated 8 December 1523 (E 179/113/212, 114/292 [part]) and one in which the indenture appointing the collectors (also dated 8 December) is attached to a similar schedule (E179/113/215A).[20] Both in Gloucestershire and generally, it seems that the indentures attached to the nominal returns are dated in April 1524, nearly four months after the collectors were given their estreats but a reasonable period after the issue of the admonishing letter. The appearance is that the commissioners had to reconvene to prepare new indentures to which were attached copies of the estreats given to the collectors, and these superseded earlier returns which did not contain the names of taxpayers.[21]

---

20 The existence of other returns of this sort for other counties is noticed by J Sheail, 'The regional distribution of wealth in England as indicated by the 1524-5 lay subsidy returns' (London PhD, 1968), I, pp 26-28 and *passim.*

21 Sheail also points to discrepancies between the yields of which the Exchequer was notified in late 1523 and those found in the 1524 returns, perhaps indicating a degree of reassessment between those dates.

Whether similar letters were sent to the commissioners in subsequent years cannot be ascertained. Certainly none are known to survive but, given the poor survival of this type of record, this is far from conclusive evidence that they did not once exist. Whatever, the sending of an estreat giving the names of taxpayers to the Exchequer became standard practice after 1524. Normally, though not invariably, the returns are rolls of parchment with membranes four to six inches wide. The return for Wigston Magna (plate 3) illustrates the characteristic format. There is no consistent practice in the sewing of the earlier rolls: there are as many sewn Exchequer style (at the head) as there are Chancery fashion (where the foot of each membrane is stitched to the head of the next so the membranes form one long roll). The majority of the later rolls are sewn Exchequer style. More occasionally returns will be found in the form of large parchment sheets on which the assessments are written in columns, an example of which may be seen in the frontispiece. The indentures between the commissioners and the collectors, which in 1524-1525 normally take the form of separate parchment membranes stitched into the rolls, are generally made into an extended heading on the first membrane of the roll or, where the return takes the form of parchment sheets, will be found written across the top of the upper sheet.

After 1523 the practice was for the lists of taxpayers for each parish to be engrossed into a parchment roll or 'estreat' in duplicate, one copy of which was returned to the Exchequer and the other given to the collectors. Normally the rolls give the name of the taxpayer, the nature of his liability ('lands', goods, etc), the value of his taxable assets and the sum due. Occasionally rolls are found which only supply the sum due. Place-names appear only to distinguish persons of the same name (John Smith of Wood, John Smith of Hill). Only a very few rolls give occupational designations.

(vi) The later Lay Subsidies

The 1524-1525 lay subsidies are generally acknowledged to be the most helpful to the historian. They are of course the earliest and, because they had a low threshold and charged wage earners, may well be the most comprehensive for much of England. The lay subsidies granted in 1543, which had a threshold of £1 on goods, have been rather neglected by historians but are much more than a supplement to the 1524-1525 returns. Sheail's comparison of a sample of the 1524-1525 returns with the corresponding returns for 1543-1545 reveals that the latter contain 6 per cent more names than the former. The increase in numbers is most striking in Lancashire and Yorkshire. The Lancashire wapentake of Layland had 120 taxpayers in 1525 and 1,236 in 1545, the Yorkshire wapentake of Hallikeld 97 and 474 respectively.[22] Elsewhere in England the returns turn out to be surprisingly full. In eight Gloucestershire hundreds (the seven hundreds of Cirencester and Slaughter hundred), the 1525 subsidy contains about 1,830 names where that of 1543 has 2,630. I have argued elsewhere that this increase may indicate a society which was becoming modestly more prosperous.[23] Sheail also shows that the number recorded in some southern and eastern counties in 1543-1545 is smaller than in 1524-1525, so an 18 per cent fall in Cambridgeshire, 13 per cent in Norfolk, 9 per cent in Suffolk and so on. How this should be understood is a matter requiring further research.[24] Welsh historians will turn to the 1543-1545 returns as the earliest as well as the fullest available to them (though they are not in good condition).

The two lay subsidies granted in 1545 had a threshold of £5 in goods or £1 in lands and for this reason alone contain far fewer names than the earlier returns. Nonetheless,

---

22 J Sheail, 'The distribution of taxable population and wealth in England during the early sixteenth century' in J Patten ed, *Pre-Industrial England* (1979), p 59.

23 Based on a comparison of E 179/113/213 with E 179/114/238; *The Military Survey of Gloucestershire, 1522*, ed Hoyle, p xliii. One cannot necessarily infer population growth (or decrease) from these figures.

24 Sheail, 'Distribution of taxable population', table II, p 59 and discussion pp 59-60.

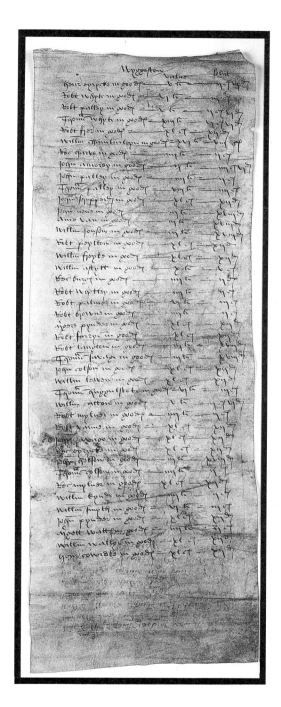

Plate 3

A classic 1524 return, in this case for Wigston Magna, Leicestershire, dated 13 April 1524 (E179/133/122 m. 4). This is only the first part of the return which continues with 25 persons paying on wages on the reverse of the membrane. All the persons in the section illustrated paid on goods suggesting that servants are not listed with their employers as at Goring. The assessment was anticipated and this may explain why the largest assessment recorded here was only £16.

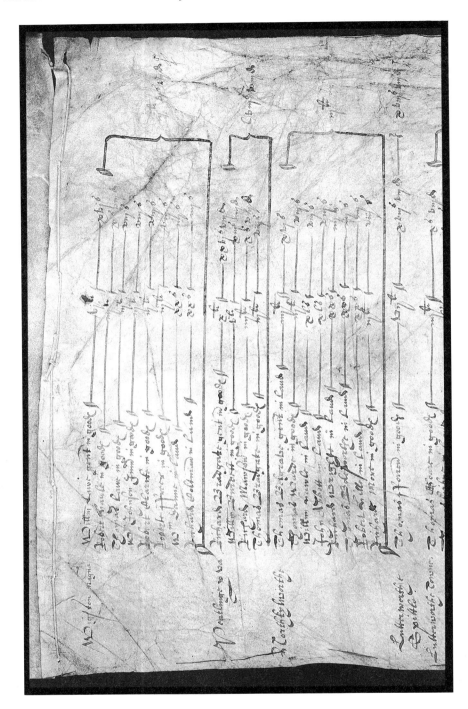

Plate 4

This is again Wigston Magna but a return of October 1600, being the last payment of the third subsidy granted in 39 Elizabeth (E179/134/254 m.8). Where in 1524 67 persons contributed to the subsidy, now only 8 do so, of whom 4 paid the minimum on goods (£3) and 2 the minimum lands (£1). In the other townships illustrated here, 15 paid in Peatling Parva in 1524 against 4 in 1600 and 36 in North Kilworth against 8. The decline of the subsidy can never be more clearly illustrated.

this subsidy appears to have been fairly rigorously assessed and the returns may be used with some confidence. This is, however, the last lay subsidy which can be recommended to most historians and genealogists. The reliefs of 1549-1552 had a threshold of £10 in goods (they were not charged on lands) and for that reason they include relatively small numbers. By the time the next subsidy was assessed (in 1557-1558), the mechanisms of assessment were failing and the fall in yields was a matter of public comment. Henceforth the numbers of persons assessed fell considerably and the subsidy returns cease to serve as a mirror of either population size or wealth. This was shown long ago by Professor W G Hoskins, who, looking at the village of Wigston Magna in Leicestershire, found that the returns of 1524-1525 included 91 assessments, the 1546 assessment ten and the relief of 1549 four. From then until the end of the century, only seven or eight persons from the village contributed to each subsidy. This dramatic fall may be seen if plates 3 and 4 are compared. In London 7,123 persons were assessed in 1563 but only 4,968 in 1606.[25]

Similar figures can be offered from York. In 1546 357 persons were assessed, in 1555, 259. Although the numbers rally from time to time, the number assessed in the last decade of the century fluctuated around 260. By 1609 it had declined to 201. In York's rural hundred, the Ainsty, the numbers remained fairly constant at about 150 between 1546 and 1559. In 1563 a rigorous assessment raised them to 222, but throughout the 1590s the number stood consistently at about 160.[26]

In part the small numbers can be explained by the fixing of the threshold for payment at £5 in goods after 1557, reduced to £3 in 1563. But this was also a society with a growing population, in which inflation and a generally rising level of prosperity should have carried an increased number of people over that threshold; yet it did not. At the

---

25 W G Hoskins, 'Wigston Magna Lay Subsidies, 1327-1599', *Transactions of the Leicestershire Archaeological Society*, XX (1938-9), pp 55-64; F C Dietz, *English Public Finance, 1558-1642* (1932), pp 391-392. The fullest account of the local administration of the later subsidies remains S A Peyton, 'The village population in the Tudor lay subsidy rolls', *English Historical Review*, XXX (1915).

26 See n 2 above; the figures are taken from the author's unpublished research.

same time it is clear that the assessments which were made ceased to represent the real wealth of the taxpayer, and large numbers of taxpayers evaded inclusion altogether. In 1589 Lord North, writing to Burghley, reported how 'there is no man assessed before me but he is known to be worth at least 10 times as much as he is set at [in the subsidy roll] and six times more worth in lands than his assessment, and many twenty times, some thirty times and some much more than they be set at, which the commissioners cannot without oath help'. Sir Walter Raleigh, in an oft-quoted aside, told the House of Commons in 1601 that estates declared at £30 or £40 in the subsidy were really worth 100 times more.[27] There were attempts from 1593 (or before) to ensure that all JPs were assessed in the subsidy at £20, but in 1621 a group of Lincolnshire JPs offered to withdraw from the bench rather than pay the subsidy at that rate.[28] Sir William Cecil, Lord Burghley, was persistently assessed in the subsidy on 200 marks (£133 6s 8d) of land, a gross understatement of his real wealth.[29] After his death his son's valuation was raised in stages to £500 in lands, but even this was but a teaspoonful of his real wealth. Underassessment was therefore endemic and, when we find even the Lord Treasurer understating his income, we may also say that underassessment was officially tolerated if not actually sanctioned.

What went wrong with the subsidy is not altogether clear. Part of the problem was that the subsidy became a heavy burden on those who paid it. The last Marian statute demanded a higher rate of tax than any Henrician subsidy, 2s 8d in the pound on goods, 4s on lands. This became the standard rate throughout Elizabeth's reign (save that it was normally collected in two portions in successive years). The shrinking subsidy roll was a reflection of the fact that the subsidy was worth evading, the falling assessments an attempt to square an honest tax assessment with a supportable tax burden. It was hardly

---

27 Cited by Miller, 'Subsidy assessments of the peerage', pp. 28 n 3, 22-23.

28 *Acts of the Privy Council, 1592-3*, pp 378, 514; Thirsk and Cooper ed, *Seventeenth Century Economic Documents*, pp 608-609. For copious evidence of the inadequacy of subsidy assessments on JPs in Elizabeth's reign, J H Gleason, *The Justices of the Peace in England, 1558-1640* (1969), *passim*.

29 Miller, 'Subsidy assessments of the peerage', p 23.

chance that the reduction of the threshold to £3 in 1563 was accompanied by the House of Commons' insistence that the assessors should no longer be sworn to present true bills. There was also a failure of the political will necessary to make the system work. Stinging letters to commissioners carried little weight when they were themselves placed at a disadvantage in their dealings with the assessors by the lack of an oath and the Lord Treasurer himself was a notable tax evader. No JPs are known to have been excluded from the Commission of the Peace.[30]

From the point of view of the local historian, it is not even clear that the persons whose names appear in the later subsidy assessments were the wealthiest in their communities or actually paid the whole sums assessed themselves. Best's account of the assessment of the subsidy in the East Riding in the 1620s makes it clear that the subsidy was then calculated upon customary lines and that those whose names appeared in the roll may have had part of their assessment paid by 'bearers'.[31]

The Elizabethan lay subsidy returns, and more particularly the seventeenth-century returns, have little to offer the local historian and are probably too far from comprehensive to be of much assistance to the genealogist. Only the returns of Henry VIII's reign are worth much attention, except by historians of taxation systems and public finance.

(vii) Anticipations

On two occasions in the reign of Henry VIII, in 1523 and 1545, the government anticipated the subsidy, that is it called on richer taxpayers to advance their tax before the date for payment laid down in the statute. In November 1523 an urgent request was sent for the immediate payment of the tax by all those worth £40 and more in lands or goods in

---

30 This section is drawn from my own unpublished work. For another account of the later subsidies, Schofield, 'Taxation and the political limits of the Tudor state'.

31 *The Farming and Memorandum books of Henry Best*, ed Woodward, p 93.

the Military Survey of the previous year (Lancashire, Yorkshire and the city of York were not anticipated).[32] Schedules, drawn from the Military Survey, of persons falling into this category were sent to the commissioners in each county. A few of these schedules survive in E 179, for instance E 179/173/196, for the Isle of Wight. There are also some returns of those who paid the anticipation, such as E 179/113/215B, for Gloucestershire. The former allows us to obtain some idea of the valuations placed on richer taxpayers in the Military Survey, the second the extent to which those valuations fell between the summer of 1522 and the autumn of 1523. Some returns, for instance that for the three hundreds of Aylesbury in Buckinghamshire, offer explanations as to why the commissioners had reduced individual assessments. The decline in assessments has been discussed for Gloucestershire, and the schedule of persons to be anticipated and the return of the anticipation have been printed as parallel texts for Suffolk.[33]

In June 1545 instructions were sent out to the commissioners to approach all those charged at more than £10 in goods or £5 in lands in the previous assessment of the subsidy with a request that they paid their tax (due to be received at the Exchequer in February 1546) immediately to aid the royal cashflow.[34]

The important point is that the names of those anticipated do not appear in the lay subsidy returns of 1524 or 1545. Anyone wishing to use these returns to gain a full picture of society, or to calculate total levels of wealth, must search out the separate anticipation returns and add the names contained therein to the lay subsidy returns. For this reason the returns of 1525 or 1543-1544 are to be preferred where they survive.

(viii) Certificates of Residence

Earlier it was described how it was a basic principle of the subsidy that a taxpayer

---

32 The instructions for the anticipation are printed in *The Egerton Papers* ed J P Collier, (Camden Society, [XII], 1841), pp 3-7.

33 *Subsidy Roll for the county of Buckingham*, Anno 1524, ed A C Chibnall and A V Woodman, (Buckinghamshire Record Society, VIII, 1950 for 1944), pp 91-95; *The Military Survey of Gloucestershire, 1522*, ed Hoyle, pp. xxvi-xxix; *Suffolk in 1524, being the return for a subsidy granted in 1523* ed S H A Harvey, (The Suffolk Green Books X, 1910), App. III, pp 402-428.

34 The only copy of the instructions for the 1545 anticipation known to me is Huntingdon Library, Hastings Mss 13886 (available in the microfilm edition of the Hastings Mss, 'The Aristocracy, the State and the Local Community', reel one).

should only pay the subsidy once but his assessment should include all his lands or goods, wherever they were and not only those in the parish or township where he was resident. The risk of a taxpayer being assessed twice or more was a real one and it was probably encouraged by the pressure placed on township assessors to fatten out their presentment. Hence there needed to be some mechanism by which commissioners could be notified that their brother commissioners elsewhere had already assessed a taxpayer or so that a taxpayer whose name appeared in two subsidy rolls could be exonerated from paying the second assessment. This was achieved by using certificates of residence. The taxpayer was instructed to secure from the commissioners of the first hundred in which he was taxed a certificate of payment which he would then transmit to the commissioners of the second hundred. If the certificate arrived in time, then his name could be deleted from the roll; but if not, then the certificate was passed to the head collector of the second hundred and presented by him to the Exchequer where it was used to exonerate him of the uncollected sum.

The process did, however, bring with it the possibility that it could be abused by the unscrupulous. Whilst the intention was that the twice-over assessed taxpayer should always pay the higher assessment (if they were not equal), there is the suspicion that subsidy payers, particularly those in London, sought to pay in the county where they held land, where they received a more moderate assessment, rather than in London. The degree to which this happened has never been established.

The certificates were filed by the Exchequer and survive in very large numbers. A few may be found in E 179, but the majority form a separate class in the PRO, E 115. There is an alphabetical typescript list in 10 volumes in the Round Room at Chancery Lane. The ease with which the certificates for a particular name can be discovered makes them of particular interest to genealogists. Those wishing to discover how many persons named in a subsidy roll actually paid the subsidy elsewhere will find it much more convenient to turn to the enrolled account.

(ix) The enrolled accounts and other Exchequer records

The Exchequer administration made both informal (paper) records to assist it in the supervision of the collectors of the subsidy and formal (parchment) records to record the receipt of the tax and the discharge of the collectors.

The informal records of the Exchequer include tabulations of the tax due, received and in arrear. These are widely scattered and when found turn out to be of relatively little interest to the reader.[35] Correspondence between the subsidy commissioners and the Exchequer is rare: there is a small amount of Elizabethan date in the 'Exchequer Papers', SP 46/27-42.[36] An item of great interest which has been overlooked is a book of c.1515-1516 giving the excuses of commissioners for the late return of their certificates.[37] One series of documents which some may wish to see are the unsorted 'books of certificates' in E 179/281-282. (E 179/283 continues the series into the seventeenth century.) In essence they are digests made within the Exchequer of the certificates received from the commissioners: they give (at their fullest) the commissioners' names, the collectors' names, the area with which they were charged and the sum due. The same series includes volumes (of less interest but serving the same purpose) for fifteenths. The volume in E 179/281 described as '14 Henry VIII, Names of commissioners ...' includes digests of the certificates for the second subsidy (1525) and then apparently full abstracts (giving taxpayers' names) of the returns for the third and fourth

---

35 *Letters and Papers, Addenda*, no 268 (SP 1/232 fos. 169-172) is a fragmentary book of arrears of c1519. E 179/241/328, 32, 272/4, 273/30 are all miscellaneous papers relating to the collection of the subsidy.

36 The calendar is printed as 'Descriptive list of State papers supplementary (SP 46), pt III, Exchequer Papers to 1603', *List and Index Society* 28 (1967).

37 In E 179/282 pt 1 (unsorted box). The cover bears an erroneous nineteenth-century label 'Probably Eliz. Salop et al' com'. Excuses of commissioners for non-assessment of certain districts'. I offer the date on internal evidence; certainly the book is not Elizabethan as it includes the *king's* household.

subsidies granted by the 1523 statute. The 'books of certificates' are an important and overlooked series of documents which reveal something of how the Exchequer coped with the mass of materials sent it by the commissioners.

The enrolled accounts (E 359) are the Exchequer's own record of the receipt of the subsidy and fifteenth and the quittance of the subsidy collectors. Physically they are large rolls, each of which contains the accounts for several subsidies. The account for a single subsidy might run to a dozen or more membranes. Each entry on the roll is a copy of the quietus given to the collector: the enrolments for a single county can be found by using the index written on the tail of each membrane on the dorse. The individual accounts give a narrow range of standard information: the area for which the collector was responsible, sometimes the names of the commissioners, always the sum due and the sum received, the poundage paid to the collector and any allowances with which he was credited. This latter section is important for the lists of persons who were also assessed in other locations and paid there. Marginalia often give the dates of payments and the date when the account was closed. The accounts are written in Latin.

It must be emphasized that the enrolled accounts give totals for a hundred or corporate town. They do not give lists of taxpayers (except for allowances), nor do they give the sums due from individual parishes, tithings, wards, etc. They are not a substitute for the nominal returns.

The individual accounts are often found in E 179 where they are described as 'accounts'. Historians interested in the total weight of taxation on a given county will wish to turn to the enrolled accounts for the authoritative figures. The accounts tend to give a single gross figure for groups of hundreds or wapentakes, but the hundreds associated together in this way tend to change over time, making direct comparisons impossible except at the level of the county. Those wishing to discover the burden of taxation of a single hundred or wapentake will normally have to return to the totals on the nominal returns, so far as they survive.

Proceedings against defaulting commissioners and collectors can be found (for the earlier period at least) on the King's Remembrancer's Memoranda Rolls, E 159. Access to these is through the docket rolls. References to proceedings enrolled on the memoranda rolls will sometimes be found on the enrolled accounts. But this is to lead the reader down byways which few will wish to explore.[38]

---

38 The procedures are described in Schofield, 'Parliamentary Lay Taxation', ch. 6.

4. RECORDS OF BENEVOLENCES AND LOANS

There was in medieval and sixteenth-century England a generalized obligation placed on the subject to aid the monarch in time of need. This might take the form of a benevolence or 'free' grant to the monarch or making him or her a loan. These loans must be distinguished from the money borrowed at interest by Henry VIII and Elizabeth I from continental bankers and merchants. 'Forced' loans taken by monarchs from their subjects were not strictly taxes (although not all loans were repaid), but like all prerogative taxes they were coerced, with the threat of being called before the council used to discipline the recalcitrant. Indeed, benevolences had been made illegal by a statute of 1482, but of the two London aldermen who stood by the statute when a benevolence was demanded in 1545, one was imprisoned and the other conscripted to fight in Scotland.[1] Perhaps because of the danger of opposition, resort to benevolences and loans was rarely made and the boldest of such projects, the Amicable Grant of 1525, was abandoned when its successful implementation seemed unlikely. Indeed, the three sixteenth-century prerogative taxes all come from the period of desperate war finance at the end of Henry VIII's reign. A proposal to raise a benevolence of the nobility, clergy and towns at another dark moment, 1594, was abandoned.

There is no comprehensive account of prerogative taxes and loans to which the reader can turn.[2] The commissioners appointed to implement each tax or loan were sent instructions as to how to proceed and who to tax and it is these which form the chief source for our understanding of the government's intentions. This chapter offers a brief

---

1   F. C. Dietz, *English Public Finance, 1485-1558* (1920), p. 166.
2   The fullest account of the Henrician taxes is Dietz, *English Public Finance, 1485-1558*, ch 13.

account of the character of each tax or loan and some indication of where records illustrating its collection may be discovered.

(i) Prerogative taxes

The first of the three prerogative taxes levied in the last years of Henry VIII's reign was the Devotion Money of 1543. The clergy were instructed to preach for six consecutive weeks to raise support for a crusade against the Turk, at the end of which a collection was to be made in every parish to finance the campaign. The sums raised did not extend as far as £2,000. Local assessments for the devotion survive for some counties in E 179; that for the diocese of Gloucester is E 179/114/260. The text of the commissioners' instructions appears not to survive: certainly it was not known to the editors of *Letters and Papers*.

More worthy of the historian's attention and a far greater charge on the nation was the Benevolence sought in the winter of 1545. This was in effect an extra-parliamentary subsidy. The commission, issued in January 1545, ordered that all men with £2 or more in lands or £3 6s 8d or more of goods should pay 8d in the pound. Those worth £20 or more in either goods or lands were to pay 1s in the pound of their assessment. Benevolence money was to be paid by Easter into the hands of Sir Edmund Peckham, receiver-general. The instructions for the commissioners for the Benevolence are abstracted in *Letters and Papers* XX, (i), Appendix, no 4 and the crown's letters to them in Appendix, no 17. Peckham's accounts may be found at E 370/2/23. More profitably, the returns of the Benevolence may be found in E 179 and form a supplement to the subsidy for local historians and genealogists. The return of the Benevolence for

Wiltshire has been printed by Ramsey.[3]

The 'Free and Voluntary Contribution' (the qualification making the point that it was neither free nor voluntary) was launched in May 1546 as a further emergency tax imposed on those worth 40s a year in lands or £15 in goods. Contributors were to pay 4d for every pound of lands assessment and 2d for every pound of goods assessment monthly for the five months beginning with June 1546. Clergy with benefices worth £10 or more were also to contribute. Sir Edmund Peckham was again to act as receiver. The commissioners' instructions for the contribution are in *Letters and Papers*, XXI (i), no 844 (printed in full in E Lodge ed., *Illustrations of English History*, 1791 edn, I, pp 71-77). Incomplete accounts are in E 370/2/23. Individual assessment rolls survive for some counties in E 179; Gloucestershire, for instance, has a nearly complete coverage (E 179/114/277, 280, 281, 282). The numbers included in the contribution are obviously relatively small compared with the contemporaneous subsidies. For this reason the records of the contribution are chiefly of interest to those trying to establish the burden of taxation on the English in the 1540s.

Attention might be drawn to one further item. E 179/240/276 is Peckham's certificate, drawn up on 2 February 1548, of the arrears of the loans and prerogative taxes for whose collection he had been responsible over the previous five or six years. In common with his accounts of the Benevolence and the Contribution, this material is chiefly of interest to historians of taxation.

(ii) Forced Loans

Forced Loans are best seen as a device, akin to the anticipation of a subsidy, whereby the crown's cashflow was eased by borrowing on the credit of a projected or an already

3   *Two sixteenth century taxation lists, 1545 and 1576*, ed G D Ramsey (Wiltshire Archaeological Society Records Branch, X, 1954).

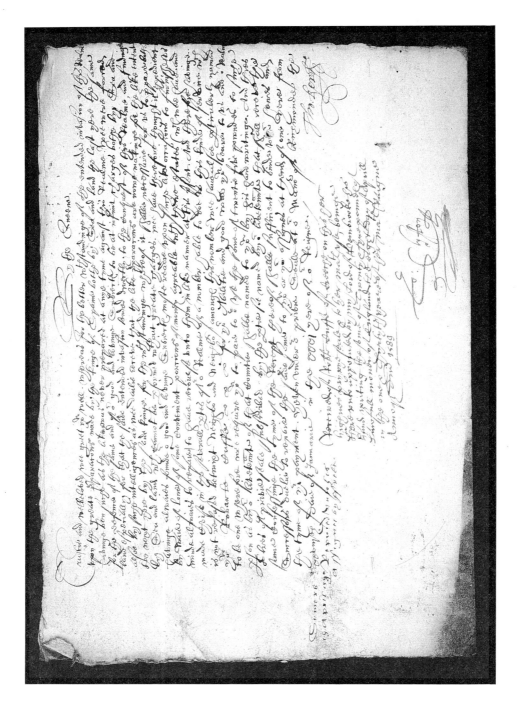

Plate 5

A privy seal issued in January 31 Elizabeth [1589] requiring Robert Cuffe of Creech St Mary, Somerset, to contribute £25 to the forced loan (E34/16). The note under the text of the privy seal acknowledges the receipt of £25 on 8 April 1589. The shorter note under the text on the left records the repayment to Cuffe's assignee on 15 April 1590.

granted subsidy. Normally the loan was for a fixed term of only one or two years. Whilst it is true that the crown gave its subjects no choice in the matter of paying forced loans (unless individuals could prove their inability to raise the necessary cash), the money was offered to the crown in the expectation that it would be repaid at the dates promised. On some occasions this undertaking was not honoured: the loans of 1522-1523 and 1542 were retrospectively converted into grants by statutes. The last loan made to Elizabeth I (in 1597) was never repaid by James I.

No two loans were ever administered in the same way. Generally the crown appointed commissioners for each county who were responsible for overseeing the administration of the loan, a county collector and a receiver-general who both received and disbursed the loan monies. In 1522-1523 contributors to the loan were identified from the Military Survey of 1522. The manuscript records of the survey and the subsequent loans are considered at length in section **(iii)** below. Normally lenders were identified from the previous subsidy roll and sent privy seals whilst others would be approached by the loan commissioners. Once they had made their loan, they would receive a privy seal which acted as a receipt, to be exchanged for the sum lent at the appropriate moment and retained by the reimbursing officer. The PRO has several thousand privy seals dating from Elizabeth's reign, of which plate 5 is a representative example, all cancelled with a note that the lender had been satisfied by repayment. The loan of 1588-1589 was raised in a slightly different fashion, with the sheriffs of each county being given a quota which they were to raise in loans varying in size from £25 to £100.[4]

The numbers approached to lend varied enormously from loan to loan. As the loans of 1522-1523 were demanded of persons with as little as £5 in goods (who lent 10s), several tens of thousands lent to Henry VIII. Later Henrician loans were demanded

---

4 See the account in *Northamptonshire Lieutenancy Papers and other documents, 1580-1614*, ed J Goring and J Wake (Northamptonshire Record Series, XXVII, 1974), pp xxv-xxvii.

of much smaller numbers of people: so in the case of Gloucestershire, around 2,500 lent to the king in 1522-1523, but just over 100 in 1544, in 1563 only 9 and in 1569-70, 27.[5] In both years the smallest sum lent was normally £50, making it clear that the crown was only interested in borrowing from the super-rich. In the last forced loan of Elizabeth's reign there was a widening of the range of persons from whom loans were demanded. In 1563 15 persons in Devon lent £1,333 6s 8d, in 1569-70 41 people lent £2,183 6s 8d. But in 1597 125 persons lent £3,100, mostly in sums of £20. Likewise in Hertfordshire 2 people lent £100 each in 1563, 26 people lent a total of £1,366 13s 4d in 1569-70 but 84 persons lent £1,960 in 1597.[6]

The mercantile community in London might be approached for loans at different moments to the remainder of the country. The queen launched a loan from alien merchants resident in London in 1600.[7]

The records of loans are primarily lists of names. It is possible from these to infer something of comparative wealth and social standing. The historian of gentry society and to a lesser degree the local historian will be interested to discover who was being approached for loans. The correspondence between the commissioners and the council (which survives for some Elizabethan loans) may supply information about the economic standing of specific families. But genealogists will find this unprofitable territory.

(iii) The Military Survey of 1522 and the Forced Loans of 1522-1523

The Military Survey deserves especial attention as the boldest and most ambitious attempt in the sixteenth century to collect statistics on the wealth and military strength of England.[8] Whilst the importance of the military aspects of the project should not be

---

5 *The Military Survey of Gloucestershire, 1522*, ed Hoyle, p xiv; 1563, E351/1964; 1569-1570, E351/1965.
6 1563, E351/1964; 1569-1570, E351/1965; 1597, E401/2590 (unnumbered pieces).
7 SP12/275 no 143.

underestimated, the surveys were used to demand forced loans, first from those with £20 or more in lands and goods and then of lesser individuals with £5-20. Sadly the majority of the military surveys are lost. A handlist of those known to survive follows this chapter; there are doubtless others waiting to be recognized in both the public records and local record offices. Whilst the quality of the surveys and their arrangement varies from place to place, at the very least they provide a more comprehensive description of society than the slightly later lay subsidies of 1524-1525.

There were two attempts to make the Military Survey. The first surveys, made in the spring of 1522, were deemed to be unsatisfactory. In July new instructions were issued for the assessment of the lands and goods of every resident person whether laity or clergy. (The instructions are printed in abstract in *Letters and Papers*, III (ii), no 2428.) Broadly speaking, the commissioners were asked to secure from each parish or township a list of landowners with valuations of their lands and a list of all the male inhabitants aged over sixteen years with the value of their goods. The instructions issued in the half-hundred of Waltham (Essex) for the first survey summarize the range of material the government wanted gathered:

> Who is lord of every town or hamlet ... and who be stewards. Item, who be parsons of the same towns, and what the benefices be worth by year. Also who be owners of every parcel of land within every town, hamlet, parish or village ... with the yearly value of every man's land within the same towns, hamlets, parishes and villages. And of every stock and stocks of cattle or other things that be occupied upon any farm ... and who be owners of them. Also what aliens and strangers dwell in any town ... and where they were born and under whose dominion. Item, what occupation, mystery or substance they be of. Item, the value and substance of every person being of 16 years and above ... as well spiritual as temporal. Also what pensions goeth out any lands to any religious or spiritual men.[9]

---

8   For accounts of the Military Survey, see J J Goring, 'The general proscription of 1522', *English Historical Review* LXXXVI (1971), pp 681-705; J Cornwall, 'A Tudor Domesday. The musters of 1522', *Journal of the Society of Archivists*, III (1965-9), pp 19-24; *Military Survey of Gloucestershire, 1522*, ed Hoyle, introduction, *passim*.

9   Cited by Goring, 'General proscription', p 684.

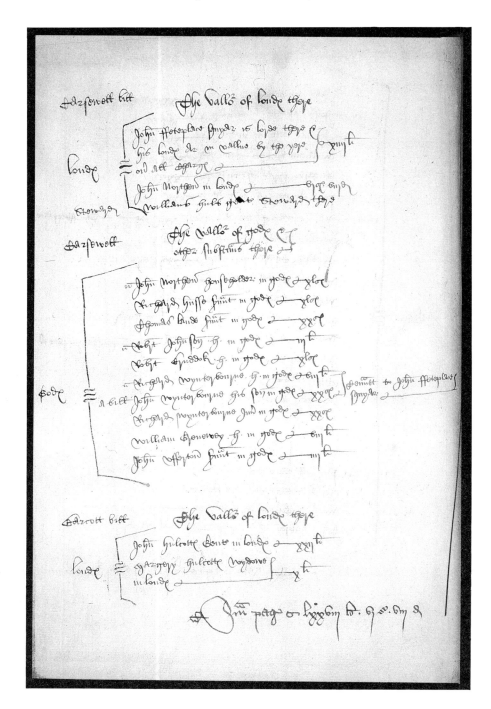

Plate 6

An extract from the Berkshire military survey showing the whole return for Carswell and the beginning of that for Barcote, both in Buckland in Ganfield Hundred (E 315/464 f.74v). The Berkshire lists carefully distinguishes between the two lists which the townships were ordered to supply. The page is headed 'Carswell bill', with a heading for 'The vallor of londes there' which details two landowners, John Feteplace esq and John Northen, and the steward, William Huls. The second list is headed 'The vallor of goodes and other substans there'. This distinguishes householders and names their servants. Northen appears in the second list with goods worth 40s but apparently with two servants; Richard Wynterborne was co-resident with his two sons.

The commissioners were then to inspect the male inhabitants and their armour at muster and add notes of the armour and each man's ability to serve to the lists produced in the parishes.

It might be added that the Military Survey was made in both Cheshire and county Durham but there appear to be no extant records from either county which might stand in place of the subsidies of 1524-1525.[10]

The surviving lists are all slightly different in appearance. The extant Berkshire returns are arranged as two lists for each parish, one of landowners, their stewards and clergy, the second of tenants and inhabitants (plate 6). In the Gloucestershire return the two lists are merged and men who featured in both lists were silently omitted on their second appearance. (Occasionally this was not done until the book had been engrossed. The resulting cancellation offers evidence of the compiler's normal practice.) In the Norfolk returns the clergy formed a list at the beginning of each hundred section where normally they may be found under their parish of residence. The Berkshire survey gives ties of tenancy and dependence; the Gloucestershire list does not. The Staincliffe (Yorkshire) 'loan book' gives ties of tenancy but omits notes of armour or military ability.

The instructions offered for the compilation of the second list told the commissioners to use their surveys as the basis of a forced loan; but it is not clear that this was always the purpose of the survey. The commissioners were to call before them those worth more than £20 and seek from them a loan at the rate of 2s in the pound from those worth up to £300 and 3s 4d in the pound for those worth £300 or more. The military surveys were then used to take additional loans from all those worth between £5 and £20, again at 2s in the pound, in the winter of 1522-1523. As we saw, they were then used in late 1523 to compile lists of those whose subsidy could be anticipated. Later it

---

[10] For evidence of a Cheshire survey, see E 179/85/1; British Library Cotton Mss, Cleo. F vi, ff. 250-256 is Wolsey's instructions (as Bishop of Durham) for the making of the Military Survey in the county.

was intended that the surveys be used to demand the Amicable Grant in the spring of 1525 when the crown demanded a benevolence at the rate of 2s in the pound of those worth less than £20 and 2s 6d of those valued between £20 and £50. Persons worth more than this were to pay at a rate of 3s 4d in the pound.

Whilst the fiscal assessments formed the basis of the loans, the military materials were used to compel richer persons to hold harness and the musters were used to calculate overall military strength. This dimension of the Military Survey, which is still poorly understood, should not be neglected although it little concerns us here. There are also extant two combined muster and loan books, one each for Gloucestershire and Hampshire, which give the names of persons contributing to the second loan, the names of those charged to maintain harness and those organized into parish contingents of able men.

The records of the Military Survey and the subsequent loans are listed in the appendix to this chapter. Military Surveys survive for some or all of eleven counties. The schedules of contributors to the loans of 1522-1523 and of persons who were enjoined to pay the anticipation of the subsidy in 1523 can be used to discover the level at which richer taxpayers were assessed in the Military Survey. These are not substitutes for the lost military surveys, but mere crumbs. They do, however, allow some discussion of an important point. Contemporaries thought that the assessments in the Military Survey tended to be unrealistically high, partly because people were boastful of their wealth, partly because they were ignorant of the hidden agenda. In 1523 the anticipation invited persons to pay their subsidy at the value set in the Military Survey. Many refused out of incapacity, as may be seen by the memoranda attached to some of the returns of the anticipation and the first subsidy justifying reductions in the valuations.[11] (For an

---

11 For examples in print, see A. C. Chibnall and A. V. Woodman ed, *Subsidy Roll for the county of Buckingham*, Anno *1524* (Buckinghamshire Record Society, VIII, 1950), pp 1-19; M M Rowe ed, *Tudor Exeter, tax assessments 1489-1595, including the Military Survey, 1522*, (Devon and Cornwall Record Series, new series, XXII, 1977), pp. 79-80; and see the comments at the end of the unpublished Gloucestershire anticipation, E 179/113/215B.

example see plate 1, where John Norman had his assessment reduced by £50 to allow for his losses at sea 'since the first levy'.) There is also a stray report from the commissioners in one county (perhaps Shropshire) describing how the persons named in the schedule to the anticipation 'will not be contented to be assessed after the rate as they were at the time of the loan, but would be assessed according to the act of parliament of the subsidy ...'.[12]

There is no doubt that many taxpayers were assessed for the subsidy at a much lower rate than they had been in the Military Survey. Whilst this may be explained by saying that the 1522 valuations were unreasonably high, it can also be argued that at least some of the decline in values should be attributed to the burden of taxation laid by the loan and the other costs of war and economic depression in 1522-1523. Whether this view will find general support remains to be seen, but there is important work to be done in collating the valuations in the Military Survey with those in the subsequent lay subsidy to discover how general was the fall in assessments.[13]

The appendix also describes a residue of miscellaneous documents bearing on the loans of 1522-1523 including Sir Henry Wyatt's accounts. For the majority of places it is not possible to say who paid the loans. There are no cancelled privy seals in the public records as there are for the Elizabethan loans, for the simple reason that the loan was never refunded.

(iv) The records of the later loans

The records of the loans are scattered throughout the Public Record Office and other repositories. Lists of lenders before 1558 are generally found in E 179, but none will be

---

12 E 34/1B (unlisted box).
13 See, *The Gloucestershire Military Survey, 1522*, ed Hoyle, pp xxv-xxvii.

found there after that date. The Privy Council Registers need to be consulted for correspondence between the council and the loan commissioners in the counties concerning the local administration of the loan. Other correspondence of this sort may be found in the State Papers or in local collections. As a representative of the last, there is a good selection of letters concerning the levying of the loan of 1589 in *Northamptonshire Lieutenancy Papers* ed J Goring and J Wake (Northamptonshire Record Series XXVII, 1975) and *The Papers of Nathaniel Bacon of Stiffkey*, ed A. H. Smith, III, (1586-1595), (Norfolk Record Series, LII, 1990).

The list of records which follows must be regarded as provisional. It does not include lists of contributors to the loan for individual counties.

1542

- Instructions to the commissioners are abstracted (but very partially) in *Letters and Papers*, XVII, no 194. For letters to the commissioners and the form of a privy seal, nos 191-2, 195.
- Engrossed account of Sir Edmund Peckham, receiver-general, E 370/2/23.
- Schedules of persons lending to the loan may be found scattered through E 179, for instance Warwickshire, E 179/192/150-152, Yorkshire, E 179/217/106, 107; 260/16A. The Kent return (E 179/124/254) is printed in *Archaeologia Cantiana*, XI (1877), pp 398-404.

1557

Derbyshire, Cheshire, Lancashire, Yorkshire and Nottinghamshire were excluded. Total receipts £109,269 0s 4d.
- Instructions for the levying of the loan, draft letters to commissioners and collectors, SP 11/11, nos 44-49.
- General account, SP 11/13 no 36.

1563

The loan was demanded of the clergy as well as the laity but was apparently not paid in Wales. Total receipts £43,886 13s 4d.
- Original privy seals, E 34/15 (two parts), E 34/42, all unsorted.
- Engrossed account of Sir Edward Rodgers, receiver-general, E 351/1964. This includes the names of all those paying the loan and the sum lent, county by county; this should therefore be used by anyone trying to discover who contributed in preference to the unsorted privy seals.

1569-1570

Receipts £52,588 6s 8d.

- Correspondence on the levying of the loan and lists of persons able to contribute, various counties, SP 12/67, *passim* (and other SP 12 volumes).
- Correspondence re receipts and balances, SP 12/73 nos. 54, 57; 83, no. 14.
- Engrossed account of Thomas Hennage, receiver-general, E 351/1965. Again, this gives the names of those lending arranged by county.

1588-1589

- E 34/16-40: several thousand cancelled privy seals. Unsorted. E 34/41 is a file of 45 cancelled privy seals, all dated to November and December 1588, for sums borrowed in London.
- British Library, Stowe Mss 165, (which is probably the source of the list published by F C Noble, *The names of those persons who subscribed towards the defence of the country at the time of the Spanish Armada, 1588*, 1886) is a register of lenders arranged by county, giving name and date of payment. Folio 2r has two copy privy seals including the Queen's authority to seek loans, 16 January 1589. There are no county or general totals. Neither the ms nor the list published by Noble includes London, the far northern counties or any Welsh counties.

1590-1591

- SP 12/236 is a similar volume to Stowe 165, the contents as follows: ff. 3v-4v, copy privy seals, including one of 21 November 1590 launching the loan; f 5r, names of collectors, ff 6r-16v, contributors in London arranged by size of loan; ff 19r-33r, contributions by clergy, by diocese, including Welsh dioceses, ff 34r-132v, contributors to the loan by county, ending with York. Does not include Cheshire, Lancashire, Yorkshire or other northern counties, nor any Welsh counties.

1597

- E 401/2583. Tellers' receipt book of payments for the loan, arranged county by county, giving the name of each lender, the date of their payment and sum lent.
- Some individual county returns are in E 401/2585 (including Devon, Hertfordshire and London).

(v) Appendix: Records of the Military Survey of 1522 and the loans of 1522-1523

This handlist is based on previously published lists by J C K Cornwall, supplemented by my own discoveries. I have not been able to inspect all the manuscripts mentioned here and would welcome both corrections to this list and references to additional manuscripts or printed texts.

(a) Military Surveys

Berkshire: E 315/464. Return for hundreds of Eagle, Faringdon, Ganfield, Kentbury, Lambourne and Shrivenham arranged as a list of landowners then a list of inhabitants for each location. The hundreds of Wantage and Ganfield (ff 43r-85v) are published in *The Muster Certificates for Berkshire, 1522*, introduction and part two, ed J Brooks and N Heard, (Oxford Polytechnic, Faculty of Modern Studies occasional paper 3, 1986). The remainder of the edition has yet to appear.

Buckinghamshire: Bodleian Library Oxford, Ms Eng. Hist. e.187, published as *The certificate of musters for Buckinghamshire in 1522*, ed A C Chibnall (Buckinghamshire Record Society, XVII and Historical Manuscripts Commission, 1973). A later copy of a lost original.

Cornwall: E 315/77 contains the returns for Kerrier, Trigg and West Hundreds; E 315/78 contains East Hundred and parishes in Penwith Hundred; E 179/87/100 is the continuation of E 315/78 and contains the remainder of Penwith hundred. E 179/87/100 was published as 'A valuation of the lands and goods of the inhabitants of Penwith, temp Henry VIII', ed H M Whitley, *Journal of the Royal Institution of Cornwall*, IX (2), (1887), pp 222-270. The whole published in *The Cornwall Military Survey, 1522, with the loan book and a tinners' muster roll, c1535*, ed T L Stoate (Almondsbury, 1987).

Devon: Exeter, Devon Record Office, Exeter City Archives 156A, published in *Tudor Exeter, tax assessments 1489-1595, including the Military Survey, 1522*, ed M M Rowe (Devon and Cornwall Record Series, new series XXII, 1977), pp 7-33 (discussed pp ix-xii).

Gloucestershire: Berkeley Castle Gloucestershire, Select Book 27, published as *The Military Survey of Gloucestershire, 1522*, ed R W Hoyle (Gloucestershire Record Series, VI, 1993). Does not include Gloucester or the liberties of the city.

Norfolk: E 36/22, 25. The first covers the hundeds of South Walsham and Gallow and includes a list of billmen in Norwich, the second Great Yarmouth and the hundreds of East Flagg, West Flagg, Tunstead and Happing.

E 315/466, ff 1-27, printed as 'Muster roll for the hundred of North Greenhoe', *Norfolk Record Society*, I, (1931), pp 41-68.

E 315/466 ff 28-61, partially printed by B Cozens-Hardy, 'A muster roll and clergy list in the Hundred of Holt, circa 1523', *Norfolk Archaeology*, XXII (1926) pp 45-58.

E 101/61/16, the return for the hundred of South Erpingham.

SP 1/234 ff 19r-36v, abstracted *Letters and Papers Addenda* no 410, the return for Blofield Hundred.

Rutland: E 36/54, 55, the first the original return, the second an eighteenth-century copy. Published in *The County Community under Henry VIII: the Military Survey, 1522, and the lay subsidy 1524-5 for Rutland*, ed J Cornwall (Rutland Record Society, I, 1980).

Suffolk: Babergh Hundred, Lincolnshire Archives Office, Anc. 16/2, published as *The Military Survey of 1522 for Babergh Hundred*, ed J F Pound, (Suffolk Records Society, XXVIII, 1986).

Surrey: Abstract or docket of the commissioners' returns for Surrey, giving totals: printed 'Abstract of original returns of the commissioners for musters and the loans in Surrey' by T Craib, *Surrey Archaeological Collections*, 30 (1917), pp 13-30. The ms does not give any names.

Warwickshire: Warwickshire Record Office, HR 65, return for Knightlow Hundred; SP 1/29 ff. 145, return for Long Compton, printed in *Letters and Papers* III (ii), no 3685. SP 1/234 ff 36-39 are township bills for the Military Survey for Honington and Cherington, Kineton Hundred. HMC *Middleton* [1911], p 283 lists what must be a return to the Military Survey for Warwickshire, but the ms is now lost and is not amongst the Middleton Mss deposited at Nottingham University Library.

Coventry, Coventry Record Office, Acc. 24 analysed (but not printed) in C V Phythian-Adams, *The Desolation of a City* (1978).

Worcestershire: E 36/35, 36. Draft returns for parishes in Halfshire Hundred.

Yorkshire: E 179/206/116, return for Staincliffe and Ewcross wapentakes, not including notes of harness, but having the sums lent marked as marginalia. Published in *Early Tudor Craven. Subsidies and assessments, 1510-1547*, ed R W Hoyle (Yorkshire Archaeological Society Record Series CXLV, 1987), pp 1-47.

(b) Schedules of contributors to the loans

Cambridgeshire: SP 1/26, ff 124-137, abstracted in *Letters and Papers* III (ii), no 2640, schedule of contributors to the first loan. In poor condition, waterstained.

Cornwall: E 315/78 passim contains the loan for the county, printed in *Cornwall Military Survey*, ed Stoate.

Leicestershire: Leicester, *Records of the Borough of Leicester*, III (1905), ed M. Bateson, p 23 notices a list of contributors to the second loan dated 18 April 1523 in the Leicester borough records.

London: SP 1/25 ff. 210-227, 227-239, abstracted in *Letters and Papers* III (ii), no 2486 (1-2), formerly two rolls, both apparently schedules of contributors to the first loan; higher valuations are marked against some names. E 179/251/15B, two books bound as one, each with original parchment covers. The first endorsed 'lones in London' on the rear parchment cover (ff 41v). The first (ff 1r-38v) is a schedule of contributors to the second loan but including people worth £20+ missed from the first loan. The second book (ff 42r-65r) is a book of the first loan giving sums lent.

Middlesex: SP 1/25 ff. 198-209, abstracted *Letters and Papers* III (ii), no 2485, schedule of contributors to the first loan, in poor condition and heavily repaired.

Norfolk: Raynham Hall, Norfolk, book of contributors to the first loan for the hundreds of Gallow, Brothercross, Smithdon, North and South Greenhoe, Launditch, Clackclose, Freebridge Lynn and Marshland and the town of Lynn. At the end are orders for the possession of harness. Described by C E Moreton, *The Townshends and their World* (1992), p 202.

Oxfordshire: E 179/161/184, schedule of contributors to the second loan, Wootton Hundred, with schedule of persons not paying. Damaged, partly illegible.

Suffolk: Hoxne hundred, Suffolk Record Office, HD1538/265/9, 18 April 1523, privy seal promising repayment and list of contributors to the second loan. SP 1/29, ff 143-4, noticed *Letters and Papers* III (ii), no 3684, certificate of defaulting contributors to the first loan and second loans.

Sussex: Rye, East Sussex Record Office, Rye 81/1-2, 18 May 1523 and 4 June 1523, 'promissary letters' of Henry VIII to repay contributors to (respectively) the first and second loans, with schedules of contributors to the loans annexed.

Warwickshire: Coventry, Coventry City Archives, BA/H/M/9/1-3, privy seals dated 3 October 1522, 17 November 1522 and 19 May 1523, with schedules of lenders annexed.

Wiltshire: E 179/259/17, abstracted *Letters and Papers* III (ii), nos 3584 (1-3), 3585; four books of contributions to the first loan.

Yorkshire, West Riding: E 315/64, ff 1r-9v, return of contributors to the second loan in Agbrigg and Morley hundreds and the lordships of Wakefield and Bradford.
E 179/262/2A, schedule of contributors to the first loan, Osgoldcross, Barkston and Skyrack

wapentakes (parchment roll, the right hand edge destroyed by rodents); E 179/262/2, return of contributors to the second loan for the same wapentakes.

Yorkshire, East Riding: Hull, Hull City Records, CT/1, assessment for the second loan, nd.

(c) Combined loan and muster books

Gloucestershire: Berkeley Castle, Gloucestershire, Select Book 28, combined return of men assigned armour, etc and men paying to the second loan for 18 Gloucestershire hundreds. A microfilm is available in the Gloucestershire Record Office.

Hampshire: E 36/19 (noticed *Letters and Papers* III (ii), no 2895), combined return similar to the previous. Does not include Southampton or the Isle of Wight.

(d) Other Manuscripts

E 36/221, abstracted *Letters and Papers* IV (i), no 214, accounts of Sir Henry Wyatt for loans received and his disbursements, Michaelmas 1522 - 1 April 1524. Another copy of the receipts only is SP 1/234 ff 223-237 (*Letters and Papers Addenda* no 455).

E 34/59 includes two fragmentary registers of privy seals delivered to lenders, with notes of their undertaking to lend money or appear before the council; a third, also in poor condition, is SP 1/30, ff 103-112, noticed in *Letters and Papers* IV (i) no 84.

British Library, Royal 14 B x, printed, *Letters and Papers* IV (i), no 972; 'A view made out of divers commissioners books of the number of able men to serve the king in his wars resident in the same shires ...'. A roll giving the total number of able men and harness for 27 counties and totals.

SP 1/29, ff. 141-142, 148-151, printed *Letters and Papers* III (ii), nos 3683, 3687, lists of counties whose returns had been delivered to Wolsey in Star Chamber.

5. FINDING THE NOMINAL RETURN YOU REQUIRE

First and foremost, be prepared for disappointment.

This may seem a rather glum way with which to begin. But the truth is that the survival of the lay subsidy returns is far from complete and, even where the class list shows that the one that you require has survived, it may turn out that the section that you need is damaged or lost. For example, the best return for the Yorkshire wapentake of Claro should be the first of those made under the statute of 1543, but the only one extant is the third subsidy assessed in 1545 and which was anticipated. The return is also damaged by damp as may be seen in plate 7.

The extent of the losses may be seen in the maps 1 and 2, both drawn by Dr John Sheail. These show the distribution of taxable population calculated from the lay subsidy returns, the first based on the returns of 1524-1525, the second the returns of 1543-1545. Areas on the maps which are blank and marked 'ND' are those for which either no nominal return survives or for which the returns are so fragmentary that little could be rescued. As can be seen, the losses for the 1525 return include much of Kent, the whole of London, Bedfordshire and Derbyshire and large parts of Lincolnshire. It should occasion surprise not that so much is lost, but that so much survives. This may be no consolation to the disappointed, especially those who have travelled some distance.

This leads on to another matter. Whilst using original documents is very pleasant, do you need to do so? There is no point in travelling to the Public Record Office if you can use the document you want to see (or something akin to it) in print. The editors of

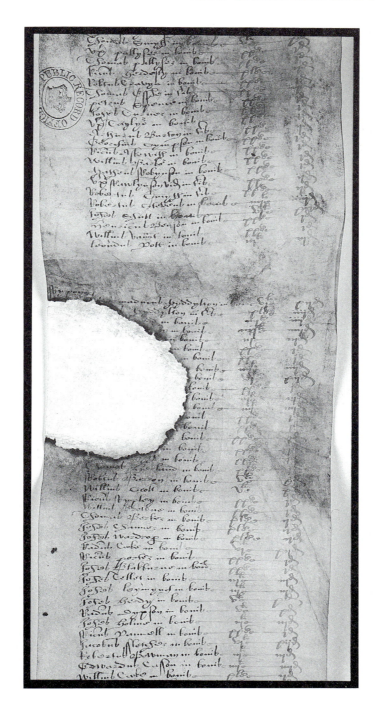

Plate 7

The 1545 lay subsidy for Claro, Yorkshire, showing damage by damp which has resulted in the loss of a section of Ripon (E 179/207/178 m.18). Damage by water or maltreatment is very common and has frequently been accentuated by the poor repair techniques employed in the nineteenth century. Again, it needs to be emphasised that the appearance of a document in the lists does not mean that it survives entire or in a completely legible condition.

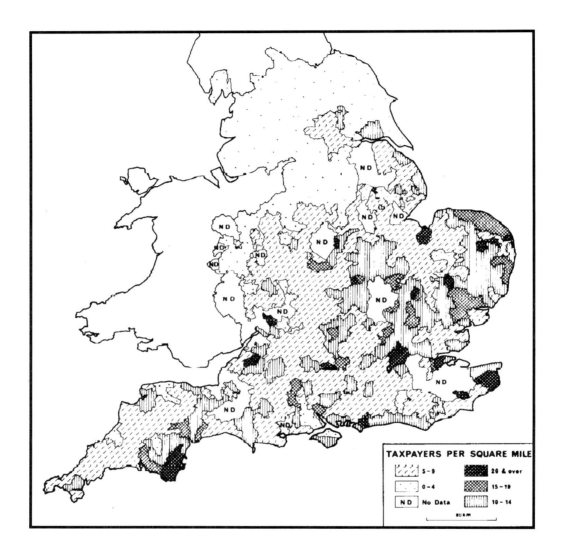

Map 1: The distribution of taxpayers as indicated in the extant returns of 1524-1525, by Dr John Sheail. Areas in maps 1 and 2 marked ND are those for which either no returns are extant, or for which the returns are so defective little could be salvaged.

Maps 1 and 2 are reproduced with the kind permission of the author and The Institute of British Geographers.

From J Sheail, 'The distribution of taxable population and wealth in England during the early sixteenth century', Trans. Institute of British Geographers LV (1972).

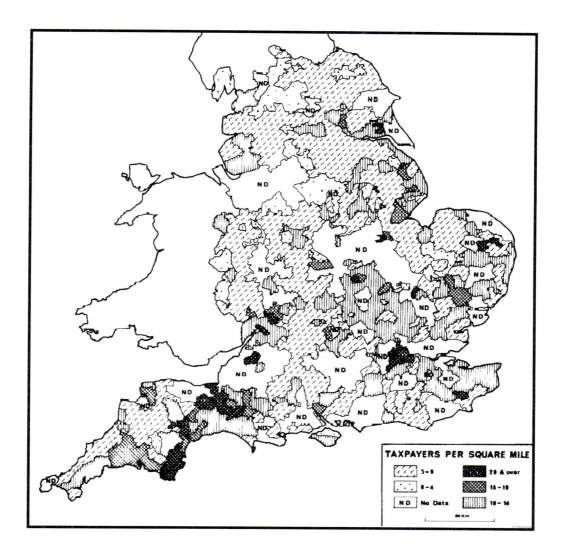

Map 2: The distribution of taxpayers as indicated in the extant returns of 1543-1545, by Dr John Sheail.

lay subsidy returns can be trusted to have pored over damaged and illegible sections of the returns and their editions normally contain an index. A list of the lay subsidy rolls in print follows this chapter. It will doubtless grow longer, but there is much more to do. Count yourself fortunate if the work has been done for you, and take advantage of it. And before setting out for London, check whether the appropriate local record office has purchased microfilm or procured transcripts of the documents you want to see.

Wherever you find yourself reading the manuscript, you still need to discover which document you wish to look at. The typescript E 179 list is to the hundreds or wapentakes. There is no index to the parishes or townships contained within the individual documents. Hence you need to know the county and hundred (or rape or wapentake as appropriate) in which your parish or township lay. You may already know this. If not, then the simplest way of proceeding is to use the gazetteer of the 1334 subsidy produced by Dr Glasscock.[1] This lists for every place taxed in 1334 (and thereafter for the fifteenth) the form of the place name used in the 1334 return, the modern form and the grid reference. The volume is indexed by the modern form of the place name. So, to discover in which county and hundred Moreton in Marsh was situated, turn to the index, then to the page indicated and one finds it under Westminster Hundred in Gloucestershire. The method is not infallible - a few hundreds were merged into others in the later Middle Ages - but for the moment it serves.

Remember that the returns for hundreds in the rural liberties of towns (so in Gloucestershire Dudstone and King's Barton) will be a part of the roll for the town and not the county.

Armed with this information, approach the typescript lists of E 179. These are available in both the Round Room and the Long Room at Chancery Lane. If you are

---

1   R E Glasscock, *The Lay Subsidy of 1334* (British Academy Records of Social and Economic History, new series, II, 1975).

travelling from a distance, then try and use the copies of the same indexes published by the *List and Index Society*, vols 44 (Bedford to Essex), 54 (Gloucester to Lincoln), 63 (London to Somerset), 75 (Stafford to Yorkshire) and 87 (Welsh Counties, Cinque Ports, nobility, household and divers counties). These volumes may be found in larger municipal libraries, some record office libraries and university libraries. Looking through them before you come to the PRO may save some time. It will also allow you to order the document in advance by letter or telephone if you already hold a reader's ticket.

The typescript lists are far from satisfactory, being essentially a nineteenth-century listing of the records which now needs improvement and clarification. A scattering of manuscript comments offers cross-references and correctly identifies some returns. Genealogists will normally only need to look at those documents marked 'names'. The habit of giving dates by regnal years rather than identifying the subsidy is confusing. To offer an example of this, the Gloucestershire section of the E 179 calendar contains three successive returns all dated 37 Henry VIII. The first is actually the return of the first subsidy granted in 1545, the second the return of the third subsidy granted in 1543 and the third the anticipation of that same subsidy.[2] Each includes a quite different range of persons.

The typescript list is arranged by county. Boroughs which were administratively distinct in the sixteenth century and had their own commissions to levy the subsidy are to be found under the surrounding county, so Bristol and Gloucester under Gloucestershire, Winchester and Southampton under Hampshire. London has its own section.

Hopefully, once you have the return before you, the place you seek will be quickly found. There is the danger, though, that if it is a dependent hamlet or tithing, it may be concealed within the larger unit in one year but treated as a separate place in the next. To

---

2   E 179/114, 265, 247, 248.

offer two instances of this happening, in the 1522 Military Survey for Gloucestershire, all the tithings in Henbury parish are contained in a continuous list. In the 1525 subsidy they are given separate headings. Exactly the opposite happens for the tithings in Bisley parish.

If you are looking for returns from 1524-1525 and cannot find what you seek under 15 or 16 Henry VIII, then turn to the end of the section dealing with Henrician returns and there, for many counties, you will find a group of undated returns. These frequently turn out to be for those years: dates and cross-references have sometimes been inserted to point this out, but not invariably. Some counties also have bundles of unsorted, fragmentary, returns which may be found in the typescript list between the last Marian return and the first for Elizabeth. If the return you search for cannot be found elsewhere, then try here.

If you do find yourself looking at an undated return, or a fragment without a date, then there are a number of simple ways by which you can date it.

By far the most laborious way is by looking at the persons named and seeing when they died, but in some circumstances you may have to do this. If the roll is reasonably entire, then you may be able to find a note on the bottom of the longest membrane (which would normally be used as a wrapper) of the date at which the return was delivered into the Exchequer. If you can spot the names of the collectors and the total sum, then you should be able to discover to which year it belongs by reference to the enrolled accounts (E 359).

But you can also deduce what year the roll belongs to by the evidence of who was taxed and what they paid. Let us take the valuation of the lowest assessed taxpayers in the roll and work from there.

If £2 goods with 20s wages paying 6d in the pound, then 1524 or 1525. If the return seems deficient in richer taxpayers, then 1524.

If £1 goods then 1543, 1544 or 1545. If poorer taxpayers are paying 2d in the pound, then 1543.

If £5 goods and £1 lands, then 1545 or 1546 (the subsidy granted 1545) or a later subsidy.

If £10 goods (and no lands assessments), then it must be one of the reliefs granted in 1548 and 1549.

If £20 goods then 1535, 1536 or 1541 or 1542. If goods assessments are made at 1s in the pound, then 1535 or 1536; if 6d in the pound, then 1541 or 1542.

If £40 goods, then the anticipation of 1523.

If £50 lands, then 1526; if £50 goods, then 1527.

The undated Elizabethan returns are much harder to tell apart because the thresholds and poundages demanded remained fixed over long periods. Confronted by one of these, your best route (if the roll is reasonably entire) is to try and match the collectors' names and the sum due with the 'books of certificates' in E 179/281-2 or the enrolled subsidy accounts in E 359 (although this may be a long job).

After all this, I hope that you are confronted with a crisp, clearly written and full document. It will, though, only tell you what it wants you to know, or rather what its compilers wished to admit. Like all documents, the lay subsidy returns are a tease from which the historian can (sometimes) tease the truth.

6. A BIBLIOGRAPHY OF TAX RETURNS IN PRINT

This bibliography includes all the published tax returns which have come to notice, with the exception of those which print extracts dealing with a single place. Many of the documents published in the older articles of the county archaeological societies were drawn from private collections and have never been a part of the public records. Historians and genealogists look to the time when all the major lay subsidy returns will have been printed in reliable and indexed editions. The present list will certainly grow: I understand that editions are in progress or are being contemplated for Derbyshire, Essex and parts of Lancashire, Yorkshire and Worcestershire. Again I invite readers to send additional references to items overlooked in the preparation of this list.

ENGLAND

Berkshire: *The Muster Certificates for Berkshire, 1522, introduction and part two*, ed J Brooks and N Heard (Oxford Polytechnic, Faculty of Modern Studies, occasional paper 3, 1986). All published to date. Covers the hundreds of Wantage and Ganfield.

Buckinghamshire: *The certificate of musters for Buckinghamshire in 1522* ed A C Chibnall (Buckinghamshire Record Society, XVII and Historical Manuscripts Commission, 1973).
Subsidy roll for the county of Buckingham, anno *1524,* ed. A C Chibnall and A Vere Woodman (Buckinghamshire Record Society, VIII, 1950). Includes the anticipation of 1524.

Cambridgeshire: *Cambridgeshire Subsidy Rolls, 1250-1695* by W M Palmer (Norwich, 1912, reprinted from the *East Anglian*, 1898-1909). Prints subsidy roll of 1641 for Cambridgeshire with extracts from earlier returns.

Cornwall: *The Cornwall Military Survey, 1522, with the loan book and a tinners' muster roll, c1535*, ed T L Stoate (Almondsbury, 1987). Merges the Military Survey and the loan book into a single parish sequence.

Cornwall subsidies in the reign of Henry VIII, 1524 and 1543, and the benevolence of 1545, ed T L Stoate (Almondsbury, 1985).

Derbyshire: 'Subsidy for the hundred of Scarsdale, 1599', ed W A Carrington. *Derbyshire Archaeological Journal* XXIV (1902), pp 5-25.

Devon: *Devon Subsidy Rolls 1524-7*, ed T L Stoate (Almondsbury, 1979).

Devon Subsidy Rolls 1543-5, ed T L Stoate (Almondsbury, 1986).

Devon Taxes 1581-1660, ed T L Stoate (Almondsbury, 1988). Prints (pp 1-111) the subsidy of 1581 with assessments of 1642, 1647, 1660 and the Poll Tax of 1660.

Exeter: *Tudor Exeter, tax assessments 1489-1595, including the Military Survey, 1522*, ed M M Rowe (Devon and Cornwall Record Series, new series XXII, 1977). Prints returns for 1489, 1524-1525, 1544, 1557-1558, 1577, 1586 and 1593-1595 together with the Military Survey of 1522, the texts largely taken from Exeter Borough records.

Exeter in the seventeenth century: tax and rate assessments, 1602-1699, ed W G Hoskins (Devon and Cornwall Record Series, new series II, 1957). Prints subsidy returns of 1602 (pp 1-7) and 1629 (pp 7-12) from Exeter Borough Records.

Dorset: *Dorset Tudor Subsidies granted in 1523, 1543, 1593*, ed T L Stoate (Almondsbury, 1982).

Gloucestershire: *The Military Survey of Gloucestershire, 1522*, ed R W Hoyle (Gloucestershire Record Series, VI, 1993). Does not include Gloucester or the liberties of the city.

Hampshire: *The Hampshire lay subsidy rolls, 1586, with the city of Winchester assessment of a fifteenth and tenth, 1585*, ed C R Davey, (Hampshire Record Series, IV, 1981).

East Hampshire lay subsidy assessments, 1558-1603; Central Hampshire lay subsidy assessments, 1558-1603; West Hampshire lay subsidy assessments, 1558-1603; ed D F Vick (Farnham, 1987-8).

Kent: 'Subsidy Roll for the hundred of Faversham, 14 Henry VIII', ed J Greenstreet, *Archaeologia Cantiana*, XII (1878), pp 420-27.

Lancashire: 'Three Lancashire Subsidy Rolls' ed J P Earwaker, in *Miscellanies relating to Lancashire and Cheshire*, I (Lancashire and Cheshire Record Society, XII, 1885), pp 131-189. Prints returns for Salford hundred, 1541 and 1622 and Leyland Hundred, 1628.

Taxation in Salford Hundred, 1524-1802, ed. James Tait (Chetham Society, new series LXXXIII, 1924). Prints lay subsidies for 1524, 1543, 1563 and 1600.

Leicestershire: *Leicestershire Lay Subsidy Roll, 1 James I, 1603-4*, trans. H Hartsop, reprinted from Associated Archaeological Society Reports and Papers, XXIV (1897-8), pp 601-27.

London: *Two Tudor Subsidy Assessment Rolls for the City of London: 1541 and 1582* ed R G Lang (London Record Society XXIX 1993).

Visitation of London, 1568, ed S W Rawlins (Harleian Society, 109-110, 1963 for 1957-8), pp 148-164 prints the return of a lay subsidy of c1589 from Queen's College Oxford Ms 72.

Norfolk: 'Muster roll for the hundred of North Greenhoe', *Norfolk Record Society*, I, 1931, pp 41-68. Prints military survey.

'Norfolk Subsidy Roll, 15 Henry VIII', *Norfolk Antiquarian Miscellany*, 2 (1883), pp 399-410.

'The lay subsidy of 1581. Assessor's certificates for the Norfolk hundreds of Depwade, South Greenhoe, Henstead, Mitford and Shropham', trans. E D Stone and ed P Milligan, *Norfolk Record Society*, XVII (1944), pp 95-127.

'Assessment of the hundred of Forehoe, Norfolk, 1621, a sidelight on the difficulties of national taxation', by W Hudson, *Norfolk Archaeology*, XXI (1923), pp 285-309.

Northamptonshire: *A copy of papers relating to Musters, Beacons, Subsidies etc in the county of Northampton, AD 1586-1623*, ed J Wake, (Northamptonshire Record Society, III, 1926). Prints from an entry book of correspondence, etc the returns of the third subsidy granted in 1597 (pp 53-80) and the third subsidy granted 1601 (pp 83-111) for the west division of Northamptonshire (hundreds of Cleyley, Fawsley, Guilsborrow, Newbottle, Norton, Spelloe, Sutton, Towcester, Warden and Wymmersley).

Nottinghamshire, Nottingham: 'A tax assessment of 1504 and the topography of early Tudor Nottingham', by S N Mastons. *Transactions of the Thoroton Society*, LXXXIX (1985), pp 37-56. Prints text of the aid of 1504 from the Nottingham Borough records.

Nottingham: *Records of the Borough of Nottingham*, III, 1485-1547, ed [W H Stevenson] (1885), pp 162-180. Prints lay subsidy return of 1524.

Oxfordshire, Oxford: 'Subsidies and Taxes' in *Surveys and Tokens*, ed H E Salter, (Oxfordshire Historical Society, LXXV (1923). Prints (pp 140-151) the subsidy returns of 1543 and (pp 152-162) 1544.

Rutland: *The County Community under Henry VIII: the Military Survey, 1522, and the lay subsidy 1524-5 for Rutland*, ed J Cornwall, (Rutland Record Society, I, 1980). Prints all the materials; conflates the 1524 and 1525 returns.

Shropshire: 'Subsidy Roll for the hundreds of Purslow and Clun, 1641', ed F C Norton. *Transactions of the Shropshire Archaeological and Natural History Society*, 3rd series, IV (1904), pp 129-140.

Somerset: *The Somerset protestation returns and lay subsidy rolls, 1641-2*, trans. A J Howard, ed T L Stoate (Almondsbury, 1975).

Staffordshire: 'A subsidy roll of 1640' [Pirehill Hundred], ed S A H Burne, *Staffordshire Record Society*, LXV (1941), pp 156-168.

Suffolk: *Suffolk in 1524, being the return for a subsidy granted in 1523*, ed S H A H[arvey] (The Suffolk Green Books, X, 1910). Prints (pp 1-395) the return of 1524 supplemented by the 1525 return; the return for 1526 (pp 396-402), the anticipation of 1523 (pp 402-428) and the 1534 return for Bury St Edmunds (pp 435-437).
Suffolk in 1568, being the return for a subsidy granted in 1566, ed S H A Harvey (The Suffolk Green Books, XII, 1909).
The Military Survey of 1522 for Babergh Hundred, ed J F Pound (Suffolk Records Society, XXVIII, 1986).

Surrey: 'The lay subsidy assessments for the county of Surrey in 1593 or 1594, transcribed from the originals in the Public Record Office', ed A R Bax, *Surrey Archaeological Collections*, XVIII (1903), pp 161-214, continued XIX (1906), pp 39-101.
A calendar of the lay subsidies relating to Western Surrey, 1585-1604, ed C Webb. (West Surrey Family History Society, 1985).

Sussex: *The lay subsidy rolls for the county of Sussex, 1524-5*, ed J Cornwall (Sussex Record Society, LVI (1957).

Wiltshire: *Two sixteenth century taxation lists, 1545 and 1576*, ed G D Ramsey (Wiltshire Archaeological Society Records Branch, X, 1954). Prints returns for the Benevolence of 1545 and the subsidy of 1576.

'Copy of a manuscript in the possession of Sir Walter Grove, Bt, to which is prefixed a copy of a lay subsidy preserved in the Public Record Office', *Wiltshire Archaeological Magazine* XXXVIII (1914). Prints the return of 1641 for the hundred of Dunworth (pp 593-605).

Worcestershire: *Lay subsidy roll AD 1603 for the county of Worcester*, ed J Amphlett (Worcestershire Historical Soc., 1901).

Yorkshire, West Riding: Wapentakes of Agbrigg and Morley, 'A subsidy roll of the wapentake of Agbrigg and Morley of 15 Henry VIII', ed J J Cartwright, *Yorkshire Archaeological Journal*, II (1871-2), pp 43-60; 'Lay Subsidy [of the] wapentake of Agbrigg and Morley, 1545', *Proceedings of the Thoresby Society*, IX (1899), pp 310-316, cont. XI, pp 101-129, 333-368 [prints third subsidy granted 1543 with the anticipation of 1545]; 'Lay subsidy [of the] wapentake of Agbrigg and Morley, 1588', ed W Brigg, *Proceedings of the Thoresby Society*, XV (1909), pp 132-151.
Ewcross, see Staincliffe.
Skyrack, 'A subsidy roll for the wapentake of Skyrake of 15 Henry VIII', ed J J Cartwright, *Yorkshire Archaeological Journal*, II (1871-2), pp. 289-296; 'Lay subsidy [for the] wapentake of Skyrake, 1545', *Proceedings of the Thoresby Society*, IX (1899), pp. 128-160 [prints the third subsidy granted 1543 with the anticipation of 1545 together with the first subsidy granted 1545]; 'Lay subsidy [of the] wapentake of Skyrake, 1588 [sic]', *Proceedings of the Thoresby Society*, XV (1909), pp 38-45 [prints the second subsidy granted 1597]; 'Subsidy rolls of the wapentake of Skyrake, 1610, 1629', *Proceedings of the Thoresby Society*, XXII (1915), pp 108-117; 'Subsidy roll of the wapentake of Skyrake, 1621, 1627' ed J Stansfield, *Proceedings of the Thoresby Society*, II, (1889), pp 62-84.
Staincliffe, *Early Tudor Craven. Subsidies and assessments, 1510-1547*, ed R W Hoyle (Yorkshire Archaeological Society Record Series, CXLV, 1987). Prints Military Survey and 1524, 1525, 1543 and 1547 subsidy returns for Staincliffe wapentake, 1547 return for Ewcross (the earliest extant).
York and the Ainsty, 'Subsidy roll for York and Ainsty [1524]', *Yorkshire Archaeological Journal*, II, (1877), pp 170-201.

WALES

Caernarvonshire: 'Carnarvonshire Subsidy Roll, 1597-8', ed E G Jones, *Bulletin of the Board of Celtic Studies*, VIII (1937), pp 336-344

Flintshire: 'Flintshire Subsidy Roll, 1593', ed D R Thomas, *Archaeologia Cambrensis*, 6th series, II, (1902), pp 141-150.

Merioneth: 'A Merioneth subsidy roll, 42 Elizabeth, 1599-1600' ed Bob Owen, *Journal of the Merioneth Historical Society*, XI (1953-6), pp 151-156.

Montgomery: 'Lay Subsidy rolls for hundreds of Deythur and Pool, 39 Eliz. and 3 James', *Powys-land Club*, 38 (1918), pp 237-248.

Pembrokeshire: 'Pembrokeshire Lay Subsidies' ed H Owen. *West Wales Historical Records*, IV (1914), pp 169-174. Prints only the return of devotion money, 1543.